The
Foundation
of Judaism

The Foundation of Judaism

Akiva Aaronson

TARGUM/FELDHEIM

First published 1997
Copyright © 1997 by Akiva Aaronson
ISBN 1-56871-108-5

Published by:
Targum Press, Inc.
22700 W. Eleven Mile Rd.
Southfield, MI 48034

Distributed by:
Feldheim Publishers
200 Airport Executive Park
Nanuet, NY 10954

Distributed in Israel by:
Targum Press Ltd.
POB 43170
Jerusalem 91430

Printed in Israel

תודיעני ארח חיים

תהלים ט״ז

Dedicated

לעלוי נשמת

אמי מורתי

מרת פריידא בת ר׳ מרדכי ע״ה

Freda Aaronson
(née Spark)

who was born and raised
in Johannesburg, South Africa,
who imbued her children
with a deep love of the Jewish people,
and whose light is always shining.

״תפארת בנים אבותם״ (משלי יז, ו)

נלב״ע כ״ה תמוז תשל״ה

תי נ׳ צ׳ ב׳ ה׳

Rabbi CHAIM P. SCHEINBERG

Rosh Hayeshiva "TORAH-ORE"

and Morah Hora'ah of Kiryat Mattersdorf

הרב חיים פינחס שיינברג

ראש ישיבת "תורה־אור"

ומורה הוראה דקרית מטרסדורף

בס״ד

שבט תשנ״ו

מכתב תהילה

This sefer "The Foundation of Judaism" was brought to me by האברך חחשוב Akiva Aaronson נ״י, a talmid in the Mir yeshiva, Jerusalem.

The author has set out to provide a sefer which covers the foundation of Judaism in a way that will be easily understandable to all. He has indeed succeeded, providing us with a sefer of great breadth and clarity.

We are greatly indebted to the author for providing us with this work, and I am certain that it will benefit both those involved in learning and teaching Torah, and be a great asset to Klal Yisroel.

רחוב פנים מאירות 2, ירושלים, ת. ד. 6979, טל. 371513־(02), ישראל

2, Panim Meirot St., Jerusalem, P. O. B. 6979, Tel (02)-371513, Israel

Midrash Shmuel

ישיבה גדולה
וכולל אברכים

Talmudical
College Institute
for Advanced
Torah Studies

ראש הישיבה
הרב בנימין
מושקוביץ שליט"א

Rosh Yeshiva
Rabbi Binyomin
Moskovits

בנשיאות
הגאון הרב שמואל
אויערבאך שליט"א

Patron
Rabbi Shmuel
Auerbach

מנהל הישיבה
הרב משה
ויסלובסקי שליט"א

Director
Rabbi Moshe
Wislowsky

שכ' שערי חסד
ת"ד 7345
ירושלים 91072

משרד: רח' אבן שפרוט 3
טל: 664-515 (02)
פקס: 665-723 (02)

Office: 3 Ibn Shaprut St.
Jerusalem 91072
Tel: (02) 664-515
Fax: (02) 665-723

Sponsored by
The American Friends of
Agudas Birchas Mordechai

בס"ד
בכסלו תשנ"ז

The author of this sefer *The Foundation of Judaism,*
is an אברך of Yeshivas Mir, Yerushalayim. He is
known to me as a person who is greatly dedicated to
למוד התורה.

This sefer outlines the fundamentals of Judaism in a
clear and precise fashion, and will definitely enable
the reader to become acquainted with the basics of
Judaism in minimal time.

This sefer will provide not only a solid foundation,
but also the inspiration to continue further.

הכותב וחותם לכבוד התורה ולומדי״

בנימין מושקוביץ

בס"ד

YESHIVAH MARBEH TORAH
Institute for Torah Education
25 MAHARSHAL ST.
BNEI BRAK, ISRAEL
Tel. (03) 6765121

RABBI NAFTOLI ELZAS
ROSH YESHIVA

ישיבת מרבה תורה
חינוך תורני לדוברי אנגלית
רח' מהרש"ל 25
בני־ברק
טל. 6765121 (03)

הרב נפתלי עלזאס
ראש ישיבה

יום ה' לפרשת "הנה הבאתי את ראשית פרי האדמה אשר נתתה לי" תשנ"ו

It is a great pleasure to see the "Bikurim" of   האברך היקר
והחשוב Reb Akiva Aaronson, נ"י, - "The Foundation of Judaism".
The author's deep concern to spread the knowledge of Torah to as
wide an audience as possible has prompted him to put in great effort
to provide an easily readable text on many basics of Judaism. He has
achieved a remarkable sefer which fulfils a need long waiting to be
filled, as חז"ל say - מקום הניחו לו להתגדר בו .

May   זוכה להפיץ הקב"ה send Reb Akiva ברכה והצלחה to be
מעינותיו חוצה, and to be instrumental in exposing ever more of Klal
Yisroel to Torah.

הכותב וחותם לכבוד התורה ולומדיה,

נפתלי עלזאס,

CONTENTS

ACKNOWLEDGMENTS

On the occasion of writing this *sefer*, I would like to thank those who were sent to me as friends and teachers.

In particular, I would like to thank HaGaon Rabbi Shlomo Brevda, *shlita*, who has been a guiding light to me. I would also like to thank Rabbi Shmuel Weissman, *shlita*, and Rabbi Naftoli Elzas, *shlita*, *Roshei Yeshivah* of Yeshivas Marbeh Torah, Bnei Brak, from whose guidance I have also benefited.

I am indebted to Rabbi Binyomin Moskovits, *shlita*, *Rosh Yeshivah* of Yeshivas Midrash Shmuel, Yerushalayim, Rabbi Yisrael HaLevi Cohen, *shlita*, and Rabbi Moshe Cohen, *shlita*, each of whom gave invaluable help and advice with the manuscript. I am grateful, too, to Rabbi Dovid Goldschmidt, *shlita*, of Bnei Brak for his insight which helped to clarify many parts of this *sefer*.

I would also like to thank Rabbi Berel Knopfler, *shlita*, Rav of Sinai Beis HaMedrash, London, and Rabbi Shimon Winegarten, *shlita*, Rav of Bridge Lane Beis HaMedrash, London, for providing *mekomos Torah* from which I drew great strength. I am indebted also to Rabbi Pesach Segal, *shlita*, and Rabbi Shimon Yoffe, *shlita*, who were my teachers in Bnei Brak.

I owe so much to my father, Reb Yitzchak HaCohen Aaronson ג"י, who gave me my first teachers and who is dedicated to his family and to the community.

I also owe much to Reb Binyomin Leib and Batya Shneier שיחיו, of South Africa, who gave me the opportunity to begin this *sefer*.

To my wife, Beyla Malke תחי׳, who is a pillar of righteousness and *emunah*, and whose family is dedicated to Torah. May we build together a home of חסד and of strength to *klal Yisrael*.

It is a great honor to provide a *sefer* for *klal Yisrael*, and I share this honor with Rabbi Moshe Dombey, *shlita*, and his colleagues at Targum Press, whose expertise is evident throughout this *sefer*.

I owe most of all to Hashem *yisbarach* for giving me the opportunity to come close to Him, to understand His ways, and to serve His people.

INTRODUCTION

I wrote this *sefer* because I saw the need to provide in one volume a foundation of Judaism.

This *sefer* deals with the basic areas of Judaism step by step, beginning with Basic Principles in the first chapter, then Basic Jewish History, progressing from chapter to chapter until *halachah* in the final chapter. In this way a foundation is provided — a foundation on which to build.

It is also written clearly and simply, in a way that will make it easily understandable to all.

May this *sefer* strengthen *klal Yisrael*, and through the strengthening of our people, may we be worthy to see the coming of Mashiach and the *ge'ulah sheleimah*.

ONE
Basic Principles

Basic Principles

1. The Jewish People

The first duty of a Jew is to know who he is, from whom he is descended, and what his purpose is in the world.

» **Who he is:** How special he is and how dear he is to Hashem. He has a holy *neshamah* (soul) with a special closeness and importance to Hashem.[1]

» **From whom he is descended:** Avraham Avinu, the "pillar of the world."[2]

> The first generations knew about Hashem, and since Hashem created the planets and stars and gave them importance and purpose, people began to praise and glorify them, too.
>
> After some time, people began to attribute power and influence to the planets and the stars, and to forget about Hashem, until eventually they attributed all power and influence to the planets and stars and forgot about Hashem altogether.
>
> This is the way the world continued until there came into the world Avraham Avinu — the pillar of the world.

1. Rabbeinu Yonah of Gerona (1180–1263), *Sha'arei HaAvodah*. (Biography of Rabbeinu Yona page 125.)
2. The Rambam, Rabbi Moshe ben Maimon (1135–1204), Introduction to *Hilchos Avodas Kochavim*. (Biography of the Rambam page 96.)

Avraham began to think about the world: how it could be that it worked so constantly on its own. He saw the sun rise each day and give way to the moon, and the seasons come each year in their turn, and he came to recognize that there was a Power behind all.

Avraham left his birthplace and went from place to place telling people about Hashem, and he taught his son the same. So there came into the world a nation that knew Hashem.

» **What his purpose is in the world:** To maintain the name of Hashem in the world until the time when all will recognize Him.[3]

In a world that was to come to forget about Hashem, there became the need for a nation that recognized Hashem and would maintain His name in the world until the time when all would recognize Him.

So we were given the Torah as the foundation of our lives and as our way of life, and the mitzvos of the Torah to bring us to holiness.

2. The Fathers of the Jewish People

Avraham fathered Yitzchak, and Yitzchak fathered Yaakov. Avraham, Yitzchak, and Yaakov were the Avos (Fathers) of *klal Yisrael*. The Avos were the *merkavah* of Hashem — the bearers of the Divine Presence in the world.[4]

Yaakov had twelve sons who fathered the Twelve Tribes of Israel. The twelve sons of Yaakov were Reuven, Shimon, Levi, Yehudah, Yissachar, Zevulun, Dan, Naftali, Gad, Asher, Yosef, and Binyamin.

Moshe Rabbeinu came from the tribe of Levi and was a great-great-grandson of Yaakov Avinu.[5]

3. The Giving of the Torah

The Jewish people came out of Egypt in the year 2448, over 3300 years ago.

3. Rabbi Samson Raphael Hirsch (1808–1888), *The Nineteen Letters.* (Biography of Hirsch page 125.)
4. *Midrash Rabbah*, Bereishis 47.
5. Yaakov Avinu fathered Levi; Levi fathered Kehos; Kehos fathered Amram; Amram fathered Moshe Rabbeinu.

Five weeks after the start of the Exodus, *klal Yisrael* reached Har Sinai (Mount Sinai) in the Sinai desert. On Har Sinai, Hashem revealed Himself before the entire Jewish people in Divine Revelation.

Hashem declared the *Aseres HaDibros* (The Ten Commandments) before all the people, and afterwards Moshe ascended Har Sinai. On Har Sinai, Hashem taught Moshe the entire Torah — the Written Torah and the Oral Torah.

Moshe came down from Har Sinai with the two *luchos* (tablets of stone), on which were engraved, in miraculous letters, the *Aserès HaDibros*. Then Moshe taught Torah to the people, both the Written Torah and the Oral Torah.

The Written Torah is made up of the mitzvos of the Torah which Moshe Rabbeinu wrote in the first *sefer Torah*. It is called the Written Torah because it was given to be passed through the generations in written form, all *sifrei Torah* identical to the first *sefer Torah* of Moshe Rabbeinu.

Written Torah is also known as "*Chamishah Chumshei Torah*," meaning "five fifth-parts of the Torah," because it is one *sefer* (book) made up of five individual parts — Bereishis, Shemos, Vayikra, Bemidbar, and Devarim.

The Oral Torah is the explanation of the mitzvos of Written Torah, and was given to be passed down orally through the generations, in a chain of transmission that began with Moshe Rabbeinu on Har Sinai. In later generations, Oral Torah was compiled in writing, first as the Mishnah and later as the Talmud.

4. The Ten Commandments

At *matan Torah* (the giving of the Torah) on Har Sinai, Hashem declared the *Aseres HaDibros*. The *Aseres HaDibros* are the central mitzvos of the 613 mitzvos of Written Torah. In fact, all the 613 mitzvos can be included in them.[6]

The 613 mitzvos are known as the *taryag* mitzvos, which in Hebrew letters (תרי"ג) has the numerical value of 613.

---

6. Shemos 24:12 (Rashi).

The *Aseres HaDibros*[7]

וידבר — God spoke all these statements, saying: [1] I am Hashem, your God, Who brought you out of the Land of Egypt, from the house of slavery. [2] You shall not recognize the gods of others before My presence. You shall not make for yourself an image nor any likeness of anything that is in the heavens above, or on the earth below, or in the water beneath the earth. You shall not bow down to them nor shall you worship them, for I am Hashem, your God, a jealous God, Who remembers the sins of fathers upon children, to the third and fourth generations of My enemies, but Who shows kindness for thousands of generations to those who love Me and keep My commandments. [3] Do not swear a vain oath in the Name of Hashem, your God; for Hashem will not absolve anyone who takes His Name in a vain oath.[8] [4] Remember the Sabbath day to sanctify it. Six days you are to work and to accomplish all your tasks. But the seventh day is Sabbath to Hashem, your God; you may not do any work — you, your son, your daughter, your manservant, your maidservant, your animal, and the convert within your gates — for in six days Hashem made the heavens, the earth, the sea, and all that is in them, and He rested on the seventh day. Therefore, Hashem blessed the Sabbath day and sanctified it. [5] Honor your father and mother so that your days may be lengthened upon the land, which Hashem, your God, gives you. [6] Do not murder. [7] Do not commit adultery. [8] Do not steal. [9] Do not testify falsely against your neighbor. [10] Do not envy your neighbor's house. Do not covet your neighbor's wife, nor his manservant, nor his maidservant, nor his ox, nor his donkey, nor anything that is your neighbor's.

5. The Thirteen Principles of Faith

The Rambam, Rabbi Moshe ben Maimon (1135–1204),[9] who was

---

7. Shemos 20:1–14.
8. "In a vain oath" (Shemos 20:7) — Do not swear anything falsely or wastefully using the Name of Hashem (Rashi). Do not even say the name of Hashem casually (Ramban).
9. See biography of the Rambam p. 96.

a master of all Jewish learning, compiled thirteen principles of faith of Judasim.[10]

1. אני מאמין — I believe with complete faith that the Creator, Blessed is His Name, creates and guides all creatures, and that He alone made, makes, and will make everything.

2. אני מאמין — I believe with complete faith that the Creator, Blessed is His Name, is One, and there is no oneness like His in any way, and that He alone is our God, Who was, Who is, and Who always will be.

3. אני מאמין — I believe with complete faith that the Creator, Blessed is His Name, is not physical and is not affected by physical phenomena, and that there is nothing at all comparable to Him.

4. אני מאמין — I believe with complete faith that the Creator, Blessed is His Name, is the very first and the very last.

5. אני מאמין — I believe with complete faith that the Creator, Blessed is His Name — to Him alone it is proper to pray, and it is not proper to pray to any other.

6. אני מאמין — I believe with complete faith that all the words of the prophets are true.

7. אני מאמין — I believe with complete faith that the prophecy of Moshe our teacher, peace be upon him, was true, and that he was the father of the prophets, both those who preceded him and those who followed him.

8. אני מאמין — I believe with complete faith that the entire Torah now in our hands is that which was given to Moshe our teacher, peace be upon him.

9. אני מאמין — I believe with complete faith that this Torah will not be exchanged nor will there be another Torah from the Creator, blessed is His Name.

---

10. Rambam: Commentary on the Mishnah, *Sanhedrin*, chap. 10.

10. אני מאמין — I believe with complete faith that the Creator, Blessed is His Name, knows all the deeds of people and their thoughts, as it says, "He Who fashions their hearts all together, comprehends all their deeds."[11]

11. אני מאמין — I believe with complete faith that the Creator, Blessed is His Name, rewards with good those who observe His commandments, and punishes those who violate His commandments.

12. אני מאמין — I believe with complete faith in the coming of the Messiah, and even though he may delay, nevertheless I await his coming every day.

13. אני מאמין — I believe with complete faith that there will be a revival of the dead at a time when the Will arises from the Creator, Blessed is His Name and exalted is His mention, forever and for all eternity.

The Thirteen Principles can be divided into different categories. Principles one to five concern Hashem. Principles six to nine concern Moshe Rabbeinu, the Prophets, and the Torah. Principles ten and eleven concern Free Will, and Reward and Punishment. Principles twelve and thirteen concern the coming of Mashiach and the World to Come.

6. The Six Remembrances

The Torah tells us to remember each day six events:

זכירת יציאת מצרים
REMEMBRANCE OF THE EXODUS FROM EGYPT

In order that you shall remember the day you came out of the Land of Egypt, all the days of your life.[12]

---

11. Tehillim 33:15.
12. Devarim 16:3.

זכירת מעמד הר סיני
REMEMBRANCE OF RECEIVING
THE TORAH AT MOUNT SINAI

Only guard yourself and guard your soul diligently, lest you forget the things that your own eyes saw and lest they stray from your heart all the days of your life, and you shall make them known to your children and to your children's children — the day you stood before Hashem your God at Sinai.[13]

זכירת מעשה עמלק
REMEMBRANCE OF THE ATTACK OF AMALEK

Remember what Amalek did to you on the way when you came out of Egypt: how he encountered you on the way and cut down the weaklings trailing behind you, while you were faint and exhausted, and he did not fear God. It shall be that when Hashem, your God, lets you rest from all your enemies around, in the land that Hashem, your God, gives you as an inheritance to possess, you are to wipe out the memory of Amalek from under the heavens. Do not forget.[14]

זכירת מעשה העגל
REMEMBRANCE OF THE GOLDEN CALF

Remember, do not forget, how you angered Hashem, your God, in the Wilderness.[15]

---

13. Devarim 4:9–10.
14. Devarim 25:17–19. Amalek led the first nation that attacked *klal Yisrael* when they came out of Egypt. Amalek was a grandson of Eisav, and thus the Amalekites represent evil in the world. It is a positive mitzvah to wipe out the memory of Amalek, and at the time of Mashiach, the descendants of Amalek will be defeated and disappear.
15. Devarim 9:7. After Hashem declared the *Aseres HaDibros*, Moshe Rabbeinu ascended Har Sinai. He remained on Har Sinai for forty days and forty nights. When it appeared that Moshe had not returned, some of those at Har Sinai — the *Eirev Rav* (the mixed multitude that accompanied *klal Yisrael* out of Egypt) — made an idol to replace him, the *Eigel HaZahav* (Golden Calf).

זכירת מרים

REMEMBRANCE OF MIRIAM

Remember what Hashem, your God, did to Miriam on the way when you departed from Egypt.[16]

זכירת השבת

REMEMBRANCE OF THE SABBATH

Remember the Sabbath day to make it holy.[17]

7. Free Choice

Hashem gave each Jew free choice to decide how to live his life, but told him, "Choose life!"

See I have set before you this day good and bad, life and death... Choose life![18]

Life means a life of Torah and mitzvos for which we are rewarded in this world and in the World to Come.[19]

---

16. Devarim 24:9. Miriam spoke *lashon hara* (negative speech) about her brother Moshe Rabbeinu and was smitten with *tzara'as*, a disease with similarities to leprosy. She was healed after Moshe prayed for her.
17. Shemos 20:8.
18. Devarim 30:15, 19.
19. Our lives in this world are short, yet it is in this world that we are given the opportunity to live a life of Torah and mitzvos. When we leave this world we are judged for our lives. The reward for a life of Torah and mitzvos is coming close to Hashem, "basking in His light and enjoying His true good." (Ramchal, Rabbi Moshe Chaim Luzzato, 1707–1746, *Derech Hashem*.)
For a biography of the Ramchal, see page 126.

TWO

Basic Jewish History

1. From Adam to Noach to Avraham:
   The First Twenty Generations

2. The Patriarchs.
   Yosef. Moshe Rabbeinu. The Exodus

3. Entry and Conquest of the Land.
   The First Beis HaMikdash

4. Galus Bavel.
   The Second Beis HaMikdash

5. Galus Edom

6. The Ge'ulah Sheleimah (the Final
   Redemption). Messianic Times

Basic Jewish History

1. From Adam to Noach to Avraham: The First Twenty Generations

The Six Days of Creation

Day 1   Heaven and earth.
Light and darkness.

Day 2   The sky.

Day 3   The seas, dry land, and vegetation.

Day 4   The sun, moon, stars, and planets.

Day 5   Living creatures of the sky and sea.

Day 6   Livestock that walk the land.
Man and woman.

Day 7   Hashem blessed the seventh day and rested.

The Four Species at Creation

1. *Inanimate objects:* a form but no life-force.

2. *Plant life:* a form and enough life-force to reproduce but not to move.

3. *Animal life:* a form and enough life-force to reproduce, to

move, and to act by instinct.

4. *Man — the Crown of Creation:* Man has a Divine soul and the power of speech, which set him above and apart from the rest of Creation.[1]

The Beginnings of Mankind

Adam HaRishon was the first man. Hashem created him from the earth of the ground, and thus he was called Adam, meaning "earth." Hashem created a wife for Adam. Adam called his wife Chavah because she was the mother of all people.[2]

Hashem planted a garden in Eden, to the east, and placed Adam and Chavah there. Hashem told them, "Of every tree of the garden you may eat, but from the Tree of Knowledge of good and bad you may not eat."[3]

However, Adam and Chavah ate from the Tree of Knowledge, and Hashem banished them from Gan Eden. Henceforth, Adam would find his sustenance only through hard work, and as for Chavah, she would have to endure pain at childbirth.

Chavah conceived and bore a son and named him Kayin. She bore a second son named Hevel. Hevel became a shepherd and Kayin a tiller of the ground.[4]

Both Kayin and Hevel brought offerings to Hashem, but Hashem accepted only Hevel's offering. In jealousy, Kayin killed Hevel. Hashem cursed Kayin and decreed for him a life of wandering.

Adam knew his wife again, and she bore a son called Shes.

The Ten Generations from Adam to Noach

The world was populated by the descendants of Adam and Chavah.

---

1. Rabbi Yehudah HaLevi (1180–1145), *Sefer HaKuzari.* (Biography of Rabbi Yehudah HaLevi page 126.)
2. The name חוה (Chavah) is from the same root as the word "חיה" (*chayah*), which means "living" (Bereishis 3:20 [Rashi]). Thus, the name Chavah indicates that she was the mother of all people.
3. Bereishis 2:17.
4. Bereishis 4:2.

After ten generations,[5] in the year 1056, Noach was born and lived for 950 years. Noach had three sons: Shem, Cham, and Yafes. In Noach's generation, the world was corrupt and evil. People practiced idolatry, and theft was common. Only Noach remained righteous, as it says: "Noach was faultless in his generation; Noach walked with God."[6]

Hashem told Noach that he must build an ark, a *teivah*, for He intended to bring a flood that would destroy all life on the earth.[7] Hashem told Noach to bring to the ark one pair of all non-kosher animals, a male and a female, and seven pairs of all kosher animals, so that life could be replenished after the Flood.

In the year 1656 after Creation, the Flood came and destroyed all life. The fountains of the deep opened up, and from the heavens the rain fell for forty days and forty nights. Only after a full year was the earth habitable again. The ark came to rest on the mountains of Ararat, and only those in the ark survived — Noach, his family, and the animals. After the Flood, the world was re-populated through the sons of Noach.

Mankind had been given six laws as the basis for life. After the Flood, Noach was given another mitzvah, since, for the first time, man was permitted to eat meat. This additional mitzvah was: "Do not tear a limb from a living animal."[8]

These seven mitzvos are known as the *sheva mitzvos b'nei No'ach* (Seven Mitzvos of the Children of Noach), and *all* of mankind is required to live according to them.[9]

The Ten Generations from Noach to Avraham

Avraham was descended from Noach by ten generations.[10] He was born in the year 1948 after Creation and was the father of the Jewish people.

---

5. See page 38 for list of the generations from Adam to Noach to Avraham Avinu.
6. Bereishis 6:9.
7. Bereishis 6:13.
8. Bereishis 9:4.
9. See "The Transmission of Torah," ch. 6, page 87.
10. See page 38 for a list of the generations.

At the time of Avraham Avinu, the people were evil and they gathered together to build a tower to reach and conquer heaven. Hashem confused them by causing them to speak different languages, and in the confusion the building — which became known as the Tower of Babel — came to an end, and the people were dispersed across the world.[11]

Avraham had set himself apart from the rest of the world. Thus he was called Avraham Ha'Ivri, meaning "the one from the other side." He stood on one side, while the rest of the world stood on the other.[12]

2. The Patriarchs.
Yosef. Moshe Rabbeinu. The Exodus

The Command to Avraham and Avraham's Journey

Avraham left his birthplace and traveled to Charan, together with his father, Terach. Then Hashem told Avraham to leave Charan and to journey to the land of Cana'an. Hashem promised Avraham, "I will make you into a great nation, and I will bless you and make your name great."[13]

Later, Avraham underwent bris milah (circumcision).[14]

The Three Patriarchs

Avraham's wife, Sarah, bore him a son in their old age, whom they named Yitzchak. Yitzchak married Rivkah, and they had two sons, Yaakov and Eisav. Yaakov bought the birthright from his brother and was blessed by his father, Yitzchak.

Yaakov had twelve sons, from whom are descended the Twelve Tribes of Israel. One of the youngest sons of Yaakov was Yosef, the son of his old age. Yosef aroused the jealousy of his brothers, for he told them that they would eventually come to bow down to him.

---

11. Bereishis 11:9. This generation was called the דור הפלגה — the "Generation of the Dispersion."
12. *Midrash Rabbah*, Bereishis 42.
13. Bereishis 12:2.
14. Avraham underwent ten trials to test his love for Hashem (*Mishnah Avos* 5:3). The commandment to circumcise himself was one of these tests.

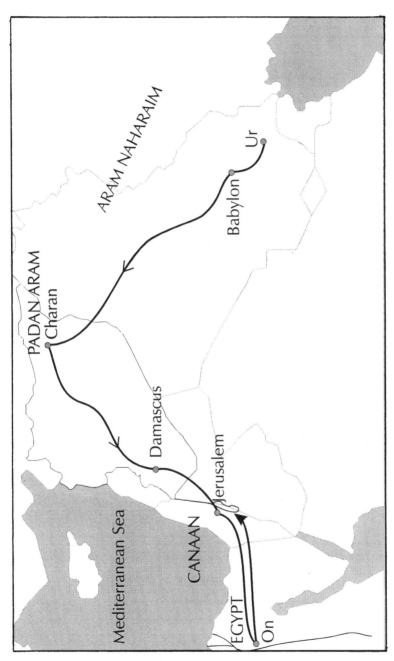

Avraham's Journey

Yosef's brothers came together and made a *Beis Din*, and found Yosef guilty of being a *rodef*.[15] Consequently they sold him as a slave to traders traveling to Egypt.

Yosef Becomes Viceroy in Egypt

In Egypt, Yosef became a servant in the house of Potiphar, one of Pharaoh's officers. Potiphar grew rich through Yosef's work. Hashem had blessed Yosef, and all that he did was successful.[16]

Yosef was incorrectly accused of acting improperly with the wife of Potiphar and was imprisoned. In prison, Yosef interpreted the dreams of Pharaoh's chief steward and chief baker. Eventually, the chief steward was released, but the chief baker was executed. Later, when Pharaoh himself had two dreams that no one could interpret, the chief steward suggested that Yosef be taken out of prison to interpret them. Yosef told Pharaoh the meaning of his dreams — that there would be seven years of plenty followed by seven years of famine in Egypt.

Pharaoh realized that Hashem was with Yosef, and Pharaoh appointed Yosef viceroy over all of Egypt, second only to Pharaoh. Yosef ordered the storing of grain in preparation for the seven years of famine.

The years of famine began, and the famine affected the whole region. Eventually Yosef's own brothers came down to Egypt to buy food. Yosef later revealed himself to his brothers, and then his father, Yaakov, also came down to Egypt. All those of Yaakov's household who came to Egypt — his sons, grandchildren, and great-grandchildren — were seventy.[17] Pharaoh gave them the fertile land of Goshen in which to dwell, and there they survived the years of famine.

With that, the period of exile in Egypt had begun.

---

15. A *rodef* is one who puts other Jews in danger.
16. Bereishis 39:3.
17. Bereishis 46:27.

A New King in Egypt

The generation of Yosef died, and a new king came to the throne in Egypt. The Israelites had increased rapidly in number, and the new king saw them as a threat. He enslaved them and ordered them to build the storage cities of Pisom and Raamses.

The Israelites continued to increase in number, despite their slavery. Pharaoh decreed the killing of all new-born Jewish males. Then Pharaoh made another decree: the killing of all newborn males — whether Egyptian or Jewish — for his astronomers told him that one was about to be born who would be the savior of the Jews.[18]

At this time Moshe was born, from the tribe of Levi. At his birth the whole house became filled with light.[19] His mother saved him from the Egyptians by hiding him. When she could no longer hide him, she made a reed basket for him and placed him on the River Nile. He was rescued by Pharaoh's daughter, who had come down to the Nile to bathe.

Moshe Rabbeinu

Moshe grew up in Egypt but later fled to Midian. In Midian Moshe married Zipporah, the daughter of Yisro. Moshe was shepherding the sheep of his father-in-law Yisro in the wilderness — when before him he saw a bush burning with fire, yet it was not consumed. Moshe turned aside to look at the bush, and from the bush Hashem called to him. Hashem said, "take off your shoes for the place upon which you are standing is holy ground."[20] Then Hashem said: "I am the God of your father, the God of Avraham, the God of Yitzchak, the God of Yaakov... Now go to Pharaoh and you shall take My people the Children of Israel out of Egypt.[21] Moshe was to go to Pharaoh together with his brother Aharon to ask for the release of the Israelites.

Moshe and Aharon went to Pharaoh, but he refused to let the

---

18. Talmud: *Sotah* 12a.
19. Talmud: *Sotah* 12a.
20. Shemos 3:5.
21. Shemos 3:6–10.

Israelites go and instead increased their burden.

Through His servant Moshe, Hashem brought about the Ten Plagues in Egypt and revealed His Kingship over the entire world.

The Ten Plagues[22]

1. **דם** (*dam*) — Blood: The Nile and all other water in Egypt turned to blood.

2. **צפרדע** (*tz'fardei'a*) — Frogs: Frogs were everywhere in Egypt.

3. **כינים** (*kinim*) — Lice: The dust in Egypt turned into lice, attacking man and beast.

4. **ערוב** (*arov*) — Wild Animals: Wild animals attacked people throughout Egypt.

5. **דבר** (*dever*) — Epidemic: An epidemic caused the death of livestock.

6. **שחין** (*shechin*) — Boils: Boils appeared on the bodies of people and livestock.

7. **ברד** (*barad*) — Hail: Hail destroyed men, beasts, and vegetation throughout Egypt.

8. **ארבה** (*arbeh*) — Locusts: Locusts ate all the plants and trees in Egypt.

9. **חשך** (*choshech*) — Darkness: There was thick darkness over Egypt, except in the region where the Israelites lived.

10. **בכורות** (*bechoros*) — Death of the Firstborn.

On the night of the tenth and final plague, Hashem passed through Egypt, killing all firstborn males of man and animal alike, except in the houses where the Israelites had marked their doorposts

---

22. Rabbi Yehudah made a mnemonic to help remember the Ten Plagues: דצ"ך עד"ש באח"ב — "*d'tzach adash b'achav,*" which in Hebrew consists of the first letter of each plague (Pesach Haggadah).

and beams with blood. This was the blood of the Pesach sacrifice, which the Israelites had slaughtered that afternoon and which they had eaten that night in great haste, ready to leave.

There was a huge cry all over Egypt. Pharaoh told Moshe and the Israelites to leave. The Israelites asked for gold and silver from the Egyptians as Moshe had instructed them. Hashem gave the Israelites favor in the eyes of the Egyptians, who gave them what they requested, and the Israelites drained Egypt of its wealth. In their haste, the Israelites did not have time to let their dough rise before they left. Their dough baked into unleavened bread called "matzos," which they had also eaten as slaves in Egypt. This was the night of the tenth and final plague in Egypt — the first seder night in the history of the Jewish people.

The Israelites left Egypt in the month of Nissan, in the year 2448. Although an exile of 400 years had been prophesied, after only 210 years Hashem had brought His people out of Egypt. According to one opinion, the exile came to an end earlier because the degree of the suffering of the Israelites was so great. According to another opinion, the 400-year exile began not when *klal Yisrael* came down to Egypt, but earlier, at the birth of Yitzchak Avinu.[23]

The Israelites left Egypt, heading from Raamses to Sukkos. There were six hundred thousand men, besides their families, and a huge amount of livestock.[24]

The Exodus

Moshe led the Israelites out of Egypt on the morning of 15 Nissan in the year 2448, over 3,300 years ago.

One week after the start of the Exodus, the Israelites reached the Yam Suf, the Red Sea. The Egyptian army gave chase and overtook them when they were encamped by the sea — and the Children of Israel cried out to Hashem.

The angel of Hashem who had been in front of the Israelites moved and went behind them, and the pillar of cloud also moved

23. Shemos 12:40 (Rashi).
24. Shemos 12:37–38.

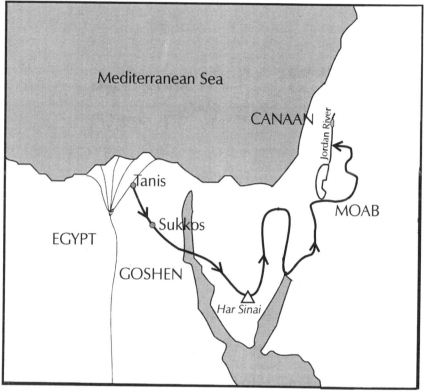

Route of the Exodus

from in front of them and went behind them. It came between the camp of Egypt and the camp of Israel and one did not draw near the other all the night.

Hashem told Moshe: "Lift up your staff and stretch out your arm over the sea" (Shemos 14:16).

Moshe stretched his hand out over the sea and Hashem split the sea. The children of Israel came within the sea on dry land, and the water was a wall for them, on their right and on their left. Egypt pursued and came after them — every horse of Pharaoh, his chariots, and his horsemen — into the sea.

Towards morning, Hashem said to Moshe, "Stretch out your hand over the sea, and the waters shall go back upon Egypt, upon its chariots, and upon its horsemen" (Shemos 14:26). Moshe raised his hand over the sea, and the waters returned to normal, and the Egyptian army that gave chase was drowned in the sea — there remained not one of them.

On that day, Hashem saved the Israelites from the hand of Egypt, and the Israelites saw the Egyptians dead on the seashore. Israel saw the great hand that Hashem had inflicted against Egypt, and the people feared Hashem, and they had faith in Hashem and in His servant Moshe.

Then Moshe and the Israelites sang a great song of praise to Hashem for the miracle at the sea. This song is called שירת הים — "The Song of the Sea" (Shemos 15:1–19).[25]

Five weeks after the crossing of the Red Sea, the Israelites reached Har Sinai in the Sinai desert. This was on 1 Sivan. On 6 Sivan, in Divine Revelation, Hashem declared the *Aseres HaDibros* — the Ten Commandments — before the entire Jewish people. The following day, Moshe ascended Har Sinai, and there Hashem taught him the entire Torah — the Written Torah and the Oral Torah.

After forty days and forty nights, Moshe descended from Har Sinai carrying the *luchos habris*, the Tablets of the Covenant. However, he found that in his absence the Israelites had made a golden calf, the *eigel hazahav*. Upon seeing the golden calf, Moshe dropped the *luchos*.

Moshe destroyed the idol and punished those involved in making it. Then he ascended Har Sinai again to pray for forgiveness for the Jewish people. Moshe descended from Har Sinai with new *luchos* on 10 Tishrei, which is Yom Kippur.

The Israelites built a home for the *luchos*: the golden *Aron* — Ark — which was kept at the center of the Tabernacle. The Tabernacle, or "Mishkan," which the Israelites had been instructed to build, was to be the center of Divine worship during the forty years of wandering in the wilderness.

---

25. According to one opinion, Moshe led the song and the people answered the same after him. According to another opinion Moshe and *klal Yisrael* all sang together (Talmud: *Sotah* 30b).

The Generations from Adam HaRishon to Moshe Rabbeinu

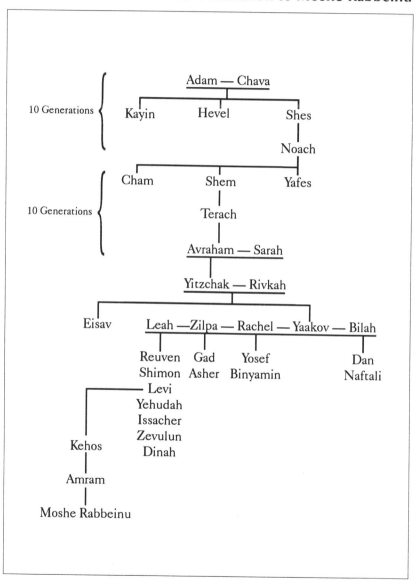

Moshe was not permitted to enter Eretz Yisrael (the Land of Israel), and at the end of the forty years, Moshe and Aharon were gathered to their people. Yehoshua became the leader of the Jewish people after Moshe, and he led a new generation of *b'nei Yisrael* across the Jordan River into the Promised Land.

3. Entry and Conquest of the Land. The First Beis HaMikdash.

Entry into Eretz Yisrael

Under the leadership of Yehoshua, the Land of Cana'an was conquered and divided among the Tribes of Israel. Nine tribes and half of the tribe of Menasheh received their portion in Eretz Yisrael, and the remaining two and a half tribes received their land on the east bank of the River Jordan.

The Mishkan, which had been the center of Divine worship during the forty years of wandering in the wilderness, continued as the center of the Divine worship in Eretz Yisrael, at first in Gilgal, then in Shiloh, and later elsewhere in the land.

After the passing of Yehoshua, *klal Yisrael* was led by the Elders. This period was also known as the period of the Elders and Judges, as some of the Elders arose as Judges in the Land. There was no centralized authority in *klal Yisrael* at this time. Rather, the authority of each Judge was usually limited to his local geographic location, while still being accepted as a leader over the whole people.[26]

The Elders were succeeded by the *nevi'im* (prophets). A prophet was a person who received a message from Hashem, either in a dream or trance, to tell to his generation. In each generation there were many *nevi'im*, however only those prophecies that would be needed for future generations were retained and written down as the Books of the Prophets.[27]

The *nevi'im* also served the purpose of transmitting Oral Torah

26. This is the period described in Megillas Rus (the Book of Ruth).
27. Talmud: *Megillah* 14a. Also see chapter 5, page 83, for the Books of the Prophets.

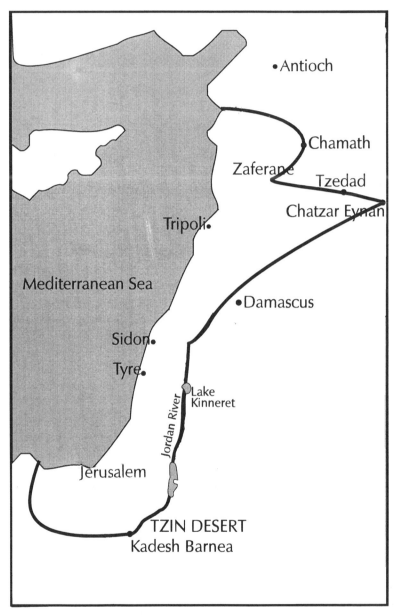

The Biblical Borders of the Land of Israel

through their generations and were responsible for anointing the kings of Israel.

The prophet Shmuel anointed Sha'ul as the first king of Israel in the year 2880. The reign of Sha'ul was at first successful. However, Sha'ul was later to prove unworthy of leadership, and Shmuel was instructed to anoint a new king to succeed him.

Dovid HaMelech — King David

Shmuel anointed Dovid (David) as king already during Sha'ul's lifetime, and following the passing of Sha'ul, the people gathered together to crown Dovid as king. Under Dovid HaMelech, preparations were made for the building of the Beis HaMikdash. However, Dovid HaMelech was not permitted to undertake the actual construction, since he had been a man of war.[28] Instead, the work was to be carried out by his son Shlomo HaMelech, the third king of Israel. Thus, under Shlomo HaMelech, the construction commenced, and the finest materials were brought from all over the land and from abroad.

The Beis HaMikdash took seven years to complete, until it was finally dedicated, in the year 2935, amidst great rejoicing. The *kohanim* (priests) began their service in the Beis HaMikdash, which succeeded the Mishkan as the center of Divine worship, in the holy city of Jerusalem.

This period under Shlomo HaMelech was the golden age of the Jewish kingdom. There was peace and prosperity across the land, and the kingdom of Israel stretched from the Euphrates in the north

---

28. Our Sages give us a deeper understanding why Dovid HaMelech could not be allowed to build the Beis HaMikdash. They explain that Dovid HaMelech was so great that had he built the Beis HaMikdash it would have lasted forever. However, Hashem saw that *klal Yisrael* would later stray from Torah, and because the Beis HaMikdash was not built by Dovid it would be possible to punish *klal Yisrael* by destroying the Beis HaMikdash instead of exacting punishment on *klal Yisrael* themselves. The Beis HaMikdash nevertheless became known as the House of David because he had prepared the way for its building (Midrash *Yalkut Shimoni*, Shmuel 145).

to the border of Egypt in the south.

The passing of Shlomo HaMelech gave way to the rule of his son Rechavam. However, his succession saw the division of the kingdom into two parts — the northern "Kingdom of Israel," made up of the land of ten tribes, and the southern "Kingdom of Yehudah," made up of the land of Yehudah and Binyamin.

The southern kingdom remained faithful to Rechavam. However, the northern kingdom established its own capital, set up idols for worship, and followed a path that led to the moral and spiritual decline of the people. Eventually the northern kingdom was invaded and defeated by the Assyrians, and the ten tribes were led into exile.[29]

4. Galus Bavel. The Second Beis HaMikdash

The southern kingdom withstood the Assyrian Empire, but before long it was threatened by a new power — the empire of Babylon under King Nebuchadnezzar.[30]

The Babylonian empire conquered the region, and the Holy Land fell into their hands. The Babylonians permitted Jews to remain in Eretz Yisrael, although they led many leading families away into exile in order to maintain control of the land.[31]

After nine years of subjugation, a revolt broke out against Babylonian rule. The Babylonians sent their huge army against the land, and Judea fell to them.

When the Babylonians reached Jerusalem, they laid siege to the holy city. After bitter warfare, the city fell into their hands. Finally the Babylonians came to the Beis HaMikdash, which they desecrated and destroyed. They set fire to the holy site on 9 Av 3338, and the

29. According to one opinion, individuals from the ten tribes returned to Eretz Yisrael before the destruction of the first Beis HaMikdash (Talmud: *Sanhedrin* 110b). What happened to the remainder is unknown. The Jews of today are either Kohanim, Levi'im (both are descended from the tribe of Levi), or Yisraelim, who are descended from all the other tribes.

30. Nebuchadnezzar was so evil that during his reign laughter disappeared (Talmud: *Shabbos* 149b).

31. Melachim II 24:14.

fire continued to burn until the next day, the tenth of Av. Thousands of Jews were led off to Babylon, and holy vessels from the Beis HaMikdash were taken as spoils of war.

The Beis HaMikdash had stood for 410 years, but now the Jews were dispersed from the Holy Land, and the land became almost desolate.

The Babylonian empire was huge and wealthy, stretching from Egypt to the Persian Gulf. But eventually the Babylonian empire itself fell to the growing empire of Media-Persia. The Jews were still in exile when Babylon succumbed to the Medes and Persians, and so *galus Bavel* became *galus Paras-Madai*.[32]

The Miracle of Purim

The people of the time still remembered the daily miracles that had taken place in the Beis HaMikdash, and they feared the prophecies of the Jews. In particular, the kings of the region feared the prophecy of Yirmiyahu that after seventy years of exile, the Jews would return to Eretz Yisrael and the Beis HaMikdash would be rebuilt.

Achashveirosh, King of Persia, calculated that this period of seventy years would come to an end in the third year of his reign. When the time arrived without the fulfillment of the prophecy, he ordered that a huge feast be held.

Achashveirosh invited all his loyal subjects to this feast, where he brought out the holy vessels that had been taken from the Beis HaMikdash.

This feast marks the beginning of Megillas Esther (the Book of Esther), which relates how Haman plotted against the Jews of the Persian Empire, under whose rule most Jews lived at that time. The Jews were saved through the hand of Mordechai and Esther, and Haman and his sons were hanged on the gallows that they had prepared

---

32. *Galus Bavel* (Babylonian exile) and *galus Paras-Madai* (exile under Persian rule) were the first periods of exile that *klal Yisrael* would endure. Later, *klal Yisrael* would also be in exile under the Greeks (*galus Yavan*) and under the Romans (*galus Edom*).

for Mordechai. Hashem had "nullified his counsel and frustrated his intention and caused his design to fall on his own head, and they hanged him and his sons on the gallows."[33]

Three years later, when the period of the seventy years was indeed complete, the Jews returned to Eretz Yisrael with the express permission of the new Persian king, Koresh. They were led by Ezra the Scribe and Nechemiah, and under their leadership the reconstruction of the Beis HaMikdash commenced. The prophecy of Yirmiya had been fulfilled.

At first, only forty thousand Jews returned to Eretz Yisrael to rebuild the Beis HaMikdash, for the land was still barren, and alien peoples had come to occupy the land.

The Second Beis HaMikdash

The second Beis HaMikdash was not of the same spiritual standing as the first, for the *luchos* and certain holy vessels were no longer present.[34] Furthermore, our Sages had prayed that *ru'ach hanevu'ah* — the spirit of prophecy — be taken away from the Jewish people, so that idol worship would also disappear. Thus, the period of the *nevi'im* came to an end, but so too did idol worship amongst *klal Yisrael*.

After the return from exile, the leadership of the Jewish people passed to the Men of the Great Assembly — the Anshei Knesses HaGedolah. These Sages built a foundation for *klal Yisrael* that would last throughout the generations. The Anshei Knesses HaGedolah determined which of the prophecies and holy writings of *klal Yisrael* would be retained for future generations. These are known as the Books of the Prophets and the Holy Writings. The Anshei Knesses HaGedolah also set the text and order of our prayer. In addition, they set many *seyagim* (fences) around the Torah to protect the Torah, and they determined the public Torah reading for each occasion throughout the year.

---

33. *Al HaNissim* prayer.
34. Talmud: *Yuma* 21b.

The Fall of the Persian Empire

The period of stability during the reign of King Koresh of Persia did not last. The continent was conquered by a new empire emerging from Greece under Alexander the Great.

Alexander permitted freedom of worship, and Greek rule was at first benevolent. Furthermore, Alexander encouraged Jews to settle throughout his empire, promising equality and opportunity, for wherever Jews settled, they created economic wealth. Jews came and settled throughout his empire, especially in Alexandria, Egypt, which became a great trading city and the largest Jewish settlement outside of Eretz Yisrael. However, some Jews were attracted by the Greek way of life, and Greek culture, or Hellenism, began to make inroads into Jewish life.

With the death of Alexander, his empire was divided between his three generals, and in Judea a new ruler came to power. The new ruler was called Antiochus Epiphanes (the Madman) by his own people. Antiochus was determined to force Greek culture on the Jews. On pain of death, he forbade many Jewish practices. He desecrated the Beis HaMikdash and erected a statue of a Greek god there. Throughout the land, Jews were forced to bow down to pagan idols.

Those Jews who were determined to continue the Jewish way of life fled to mountain caves in the desert, led by the priestly family of Chashmonai, the Hasmoneans. The Greek army was huge and powerful, but the Jews, under Yehudah HaMaccabee, defeated Antiochus and drove the Greeks from the land, at first from the south of the country and then out of the land altogether.

Following the recapture of Judea, the Jews came to the Beis HaMikdash and cleansed and purified the Holy Site. On the twenty-fifth of Kislev they rekindled the lights in the courtyard of the Sanctuary. However, they were only able to find one jar with the seal of the *kohen gadol* still intact. The quantity was sufficient to last for only one day, but instead lasted for eight days. Chanukah commemorates the miracles of that time; our Sages established these eight days of Chanukah as days of praise and thanksgiving to Hashem.[35]

35. Talmud: *Shabbos* 21b.

Chanukah means "dedication," as it was the time when the Beis HaMikdash was rededicated to the service of Hashem.

5. Galus Edom

The Maccabean era lasted for seventy years under the rule of the Hasmonean princes, who held Judea together and restored the Torah way of life.

However, the period of peace was not to last, for the growing empire of Rome began to make inroads into the region. The Romans finally dominated the region, bringing the Greek era to a close.

Judea came under the rule of Rome in 3697, when Pompeii captured the land, killing thousands and placing a heavy tax burden on the people. The Romans ruled through procurators, who had little sympathy for the population.

At first the oppression was political and economic. In internal affairs the Jews were permitted freedom of worship, and the service in the Beis HaMikdash continued. However, with the reign of Emperor Tiberias the situation changed, and persecution of the Jews began. This led to many revolts against Roman rule, until in 3826 a major revolt broke out led by a group known as "Zealots." They captured many key positions in the country and eventually defeated the Roman garrison that was stationed in Jerusalem, taking control of the city. Eventually, through a campaign of guerilla warfare, they drove the Romans from Judea.

Emperor Nero sent his most able general, Vespasian, to quell the revolt. By this time the Romans knew how to deal with guerilla warfare, and they laid siege to the zealot strongholds throughout the land. The stronghold of the Galilee was the first to fall to the Romans, followed by the fall of other strongholds. Then the Romans turned to Jerusalem and laid siege to the holy city.

The Romans had a sophisticated army, but the city was well fortified and supplied with provisions, and they were able to hold out against siege. The Romans planned to make an agreement with the Jews, but it became clear that internal strife within the city was weakening the ability of the defenders to resist. The Romans resolved to continue the siege.

The sage Rabbi Yochanan ben Zakkai saw that the situation was becoming hopeless and decided to salvage what he could out of the impending destruction. He had a rumor spread that he had become ill and, later, that he had passed away. Thus his students were permitted to carry him out of the city in a coffin for burial.

Once out of the city, Rabbi Yochanan made his way to Vespasian and greeted him as Emperor of Rome. The general was surprised to be greeted this way, but while they were together, a messenger arrived to tell him that he had indeed been elected emperor following the death of Nero. Vespasian was impressed by the great sage and granted him three requests. Rabbi Yochanan asked that the Romans spare the yeshivah at Yavneh and its Sages; that the princely lineage (descending from Hillel) should be spared; and that a physician heal the old sage Rabbi Tzadok, who had fasted for forty years in his attempt to save Jerusalem.[36]

Vespasian then returned to Rome as emperor, leaving his son Titus to take over the siege of Jerusalem.

The Romans continued the siege in brutal warfare. Eventually, on 17 Tammuz 3828, they breached the outer walls of the city. Inside Jerusalem, thousands were dying, not only through warfare but also due to hunger, as internal conflict had led to the depletion of food stocks.

Eventually the inner walls of Jerusalem also fell. The Romans were now able to make their way to the Beis HaMikdash. They desecrated and destroyed the Holy Site, and on 9 Av 3828, they set the Beis HaMikdash on fire. The fire continued to burn until the next day, the tenth of Av. It had been three weeks since the Romans had first breached the walls of the city.[37]

Approximately one million Jews lost their lives during the siege of Jerusalem, and in addition tens of thousands were led to Rome as slaves. Holy vessels from the Beis HaMikdash were taken to Rome as spoils of war, and the procession that entered Rome was recorded

---

36. Talmud: *Gittin* 56b.
37. This three-week period is marked each year by three weeks of mourning in the Jewish calendar, called "the Three Weeks."

on the Arch of Titus, built to commemorate the victory. In Rome, Vespasian minted coins marked with the words *"Judea Capta."*

In 3831, three years after the fall of Jerusalem, one of the last areas of resistance was crushed at the mountain fortress of Masada, a natural desert fortress which had been fortified by Herod as his winter palace.

Now the Romans set out to force Jews to adopt Roman religion and culture and issued harsh decrees against the Jews. They forbade many Jewish practices, until, eventually, sixty-four years after the fall of Jerusalem, a revolt broke out led by Bar Kochba and under the spiritual leadership of Rabbi Akiva. Under Bar Kochba, the Roman legions were driven from the land.

Emperor Hadrian summoned Julius Severus from Britain to retake Judea, and Severus brought with him the Roman legions stationed in Britain. Severus isolated the rebels, cut off their supplies, and starved them out. Despite heavy losses, the Romans defeated Bar Kochba at Betar in 3896. The defeat at Betar was the final defeat in the Bar Kochba revolt.

The revolt of Bar Kochba had lasted three and half years and cost six hundred thousand lives, and in the end, Judea had become almost a desert.

In the years that followed the revolt, many of the greatest Jewish Sages were captured and cruelly murdered by the Romans. These Sages are known as the *"aseres harugei malchus,"* the ten martyrs slain by the Romans.

Jews were no longer allowed into Jerusalem, and a temple to a Roman god was erected where the Beis HaMikdash once stood. Many Jews left the Holy Land for communities in Babylon and around the Mediterranean, which had developed since the time of the first Beis HaMikdash.

As this period of exile continued, the Roman Empire continued to grow stronger and stronger, and the Jews became dispersed across many lands, under greater foreign influence than ever before. The quality of Jewish learning declined, and the Sages feared for the continued transmission of Torah.[38]

---

38. Rambam: Introduction to Commentary on the Mishnah.

At this time, the Jewish people were led by Rabbi Yehudah HaNasi, or Rebi, as he was known. Rebi was both the spiritual leader of the Jewish people and the leader of the Jewish state vis à vis the Roman Empire. Together with the Sages of his generation, Rebi set out to compile in writing a framework of Oral Torah to serve as a foundation for future generations. Although it was forbidden to write down Oral Torah, the Sages acted on the basis of the rule 'עת לעשות לה — "Time to act for Hashem" (Tehillim 119:126).

This compilation was the work of a lifetime for Rebi and his Sages, and it became known as the Mishnah, meaning "a teaching." Rebi and his Sages, who were the last of the generations called "Tannaim," had written down publicly, for the first time, a framework and foundation on which Oral Torah would rest.

In the years that followed the sealing of the Mishnah, great yeshivos were established in Babylon by the students of Rebi. In Eretz Yisrael, the population continued to decline because of the difficulty of life under Roman rule, and by the time the last communities had to leave the Land, there were already flourishing communities in Babylon.

About two hundred and fifty years after the sealing of the Mishnah, Ravina and Rav Ashi, the last of the Amoraim, began the task of collating and editing all the discussions of the Amoraim, which led from the Mishnah, which had been passed down through the generations before them.

Ravina and Rav Ashi were the great *roshei yeshivah* of their generation, and this compilation, too, was the work of a lifetime for them and their students. This work became known as *"Talmud Bavli,"* or simply as "the Talmud," the central pillar of Jewish learning.

In Eretz Yisrael, too, a Talmud had been compiled by the Sages of Eretz Yisrael called *Talmud Yerushalmi.*

For another three hundred years after the destruction of the Second Beis HaMikdash, the Roman Empire continued to expand, until it was divided into two halves: the Western Empire in the west and the Byzantine Empire in the east. The Byzantine Empire became dominated by Muslim culture, and the Western Empire became divided among European tribes whose territory later emerged as

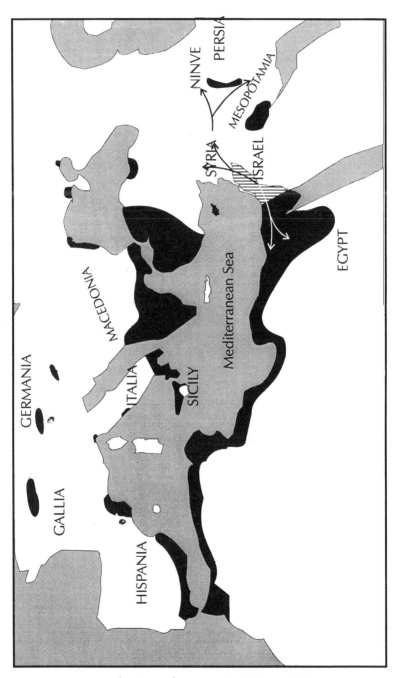

Jewish Population 2,488–4,500

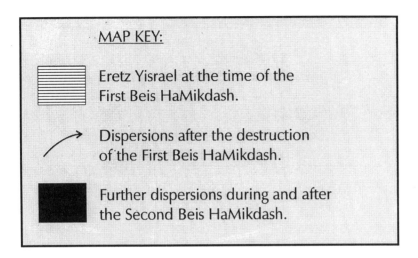

MAP KEY:

Eretz Yisrael at the time of the
First Beis HaMikdash.

Dispersions after the destruction
of the First Beis HaMikdash.

Further dispersions during and after
the Second Beis HaMikdash.

independent kingdoms, and eventually the nation states of today.

Across Europe are architectural remains from the period 2,000 years ago when Rome rose to dominate Europe.

The Last Twelve Hundred Years

About twelve hundred years ago Jews began to migrate up from the Mediterranean lands, north-eastward through Europe. They fled persecution, seeking security and opportunity elsewhere. Those Jews who remained in the Mediterranean and Asian lands became known as Sephardi (meaning Spanish) Jews, although by no means did all Sephardi Jews live in Spain. Those who migrated up through Europe became known as Ashkenazi (meaning German) Jews, although the largest communities of Ashkenazi Jews would later be further east, particularly in Poland and Russia.

Thus, over a period of hundreds of years, Ashkenazi Jews migrated up through Europe, building communities wherever they settled, eventually absorbing German as their language and taking it with them as Yiddish into new lands as they migrated.

Migration of Ashkenazi Jews over the last 1200 years

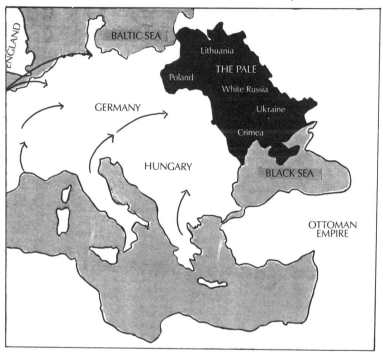

Most Russian Jews were forced to live in the Pale of Settlement.
Between 1835–1914 over four million Jews lived there.

By the end of the sixteenth century, there were large areas of Jewish settlement in Poland. Jews were encouraged to come and settle in Poland. The Polish barons wanted Jews to develop Poland's economy and offered them freedom of religion and security. The Jews came, and these lands became areas of great Jewish settlement and learning, the beginning of Jewish settlement in Eastern Europe that would last for five hundred years.

Although this had been a period of great productivity in Jewish life, no community was long safe from persecution, and in almost every generation Jews were forced to flee their homes. In particular, the Crusades from 1096 onwards devastated Jewish communities, and there were pogroms and expulsions almost everywhere in Europe.[39]

Between the years 1347–1350, the Jewish communities of Europe also suffered in the wake of the Black Death. The Black Death was a plague transmitted on board merchant ships from Asia, which in the space of a few years swept Europe, killing a third of Europe's inhabitants. Jews survived the plague better than others and were blamed for causing it, sparking pogroms across Europe.

The Jews of Europe were also to suffer at the hands of the Cossacks under Bogdan Chmielnicki. In 1648 the Cossacks were united under Chmielnicki, and for nearly the next ten years they ravaged Eastern Europe, devastating Jewish communities. These massacres became known as the massacres of *Tach veTat*.[40]

Shortly after the end of the Chmielnicki massacres there appeared a man amongst *klal Yisrael* who proclaimed himself to be the Mashiach. This man was called Shabbetai Tzvi. Shabbetai Tzvi

---

39. The Crusades were "Holy Wars," called to liberate the Holy Land from Arab hands. The Crusaders made up massive hordes which rampaged through Europe on their way to the Holy Land, devastating Jewish communities and destroying many altogether.

40. In Hebrew, the letters תח (*tach*) and טט (*tat*) have the numerical values 408 and 409 respectively, meaning the years 5408 and 5409. These correspond to the years 1648–1649 in the secular calendar.

was a gifted, charismatic person who in this period of turmoil convinced many that he was indeed Mashiach. When he was eventually exposed, there was dismay in many parts of the Jewish world.

However, in the year 1698, a new light came into the Jewish world. He was Yisrael ben Eliezer, who became known as the Baal Shem Tov, the "Master of the Good Name." Even as a young man, the Baal Shem Tov was known as a healer and holy man, and as he crossed the provinces of Poland and the Ukraine he began to draw many followers. The followers of the Baal Shem Tov became known as Chassidim, meaning "pious ones." The offspring and *talmidim* of the Baal Shem Tov included many great scholars who were to become founders of chassidic dynasties across Eastern Europe, particularly Poland, the Ukraine, and Hungary.[41]

By the time the Baal Shem Tov passed away on Shavuos 1760, Chassidism had begun a new dimension and revitalization of much of Eastern European Jewry.

In Eastern Europe the lives of Jews were simple. Jews lived in *shtetlach*, small impoverished towns, where they earned their living as artisans and traders. Jews were not forced to live in these areas, but where Jews lived, the towns were predominantly Jewish. In Russia, however, under the last czars, Jews were restricted to living within the Pale of Settlement, along the western border of Russia. Under the last czars, too, there was a drift to the larger towns within "the Pale."

---

41. One of the grandsons of the Baal Shem Tov was Rabbi Baruch of Mezibuzh and another of his grandsons was Rabbi Nachman of Breslov, the founder of Breslov Chassidim. The principle pupil of the Baal Shem Tov was Rabbi Dov Ber of Mezeritch, known as the Maggid of Mezeritch. The Maggid of Mezeritch reared the next generation of the leaders of Chassidism, including the brothers Rabbi Pinchas HaLevi Horovitz and Rabbi Shmelke of Nicholsburg; Rabbi Aharon Perlow of Karlin; the brothers Rabbi Elimelech of Lizhensk and Rabbi Zusia of Hanipoli; Rabbi Nachum Twersky of Chernobyl; Rabbi Abraham of Kalisk; Rabbi Levi Yitzchak of Berdichev; Rabbi Shneur Zalman of Liadi, founder of Chabad Chassidus; Rabbi Yisroel of Kozhnitz; and Rabbi Avraham Yehoshua Heschel of Apt. These great leaders, their sons, and *talmidim* firmly established Chassidus across Eastern European Jewry.

In the countries in Western Europe, however, the pattern of life was different. These lands were comparatively wealthy, and particularly in Germany, society was more organized and centered in towns.

The French revolution in 1789 brought changes in society, initially in France and then gradually in other parts of Europe, breaking down the previous forms of society. In addition, the Industrial Revolution, which started moving across Europe from the west about two hundred years ago, brought with it great changes in the lives of the people of Europe. Great industrial and commercial centers began to develop, and people were attracted away from the countryside to the towns.

These changes in society brought with them the movements of emancipation that swept Western Europe. For the Jews of these lands, barriers came down between Jew and gentile, and Jews became involved in their new society.

The Industrial Revolution, however, took longer to reach Eastern Europe, and there the lives of the Jews remained largely unchanged.

During this period of Ashkenazi migration up through Europe, great communities had also developed in Sephardi lands. In these Mediterranean lands, Spain had become the crown of the Sephardi world. There were also important Sephardi communities around the Mediterranean, in Italy, Turkey, and Arab North African lands. Sephardi communities had also developed as far as India and Asia.

In Spain, however, in 1469, the different kingdoms had become united under Ferdinand and Isabella, and in 1492 they issued a decree expelling all Jews from Spain. The Expulsion brought to an end the glorious era of Spanish Jewry, and Spanish Jews were forced to flee to wherever they could find refuge. Their distinguished communities disappeared, but they transplanted their learning and culture onto new soil, building up important communities in North Africa, the Ottoman Empire, Italy, and Holland.

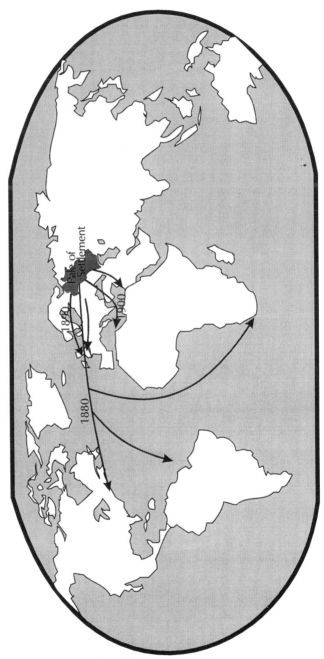

Migration of Ashkenazi Jews 1880 –1939

The Last One Hundred Years

Between the years 1880–1939, there was a huge emigration of Jews from Europe. At first, Jews fled from Eastern Europe, driven by pogroms and persecution under the czars. During this period, over two million Jews left just from the Pale of Settlement alone. From the 1930s onwards Jews began to flee from Western Europe, too. Jews went to America, England, South Africa, Eretz Yisrael, and finally to wherever they could find a place that would take them. Of those who remained, few survived.

In 1933 a dictator came to power in Germany who was openly against the Jews, and who brought upon the world the Second World War and together with it the holocaust of European Jewry. The Holocaust was the greatest loss of Jewish life in history, which brought to an end Jewish life in most of Europe.

For the Jews of Arab lands, the intense anti-semitism of Europe remained distant, although in these lands, too, Jews were persecuted and segregated from the rest of society. In recent decades anti-Jewish sentiment in these lands has caused most Jews to emigrate.

Outline of Great Sages of the Jewish People[42]

Great Sages of the Jewish people from the period of the Second Beis HaMikdash, over two thousand years ago:

Tannaim. Eretz Yisrael 3500–3950

The Tannaim of Eretz Yisrael include Rabbi Yochanan ben Zakkai, Rabbi Eliezer ben Hyrkanos, Rabbi Yehoshua ben Chananina, Rabbi Yose HaCohen, Rabbi Shimon ben Nesanel, Rabbi Elazar ben Arach, Rabban Gamliel II, Rabbi Akiva, Rabbi Tarfon, Rabbi Yishmael II, Rabban Shimon III, Rabban Shimon bar Yochai, Rabbi Yehudah HaNossi.

---

42. For a more detailed history, see chapter six.

Amoraim. Eretz Yisrael 3950-4100

The Amoraim of Eretz Yisrael include Rabban Gamliel III (son of Rabbi Yehudah HaNossi), Rabbi Yochanan ben Nafcha, Rabbi Shimon ben Lakish (Resh Lakish), Rabbi Yehudah II Nessiah, Rabbi Elazar ben Pedas, Rabbi Abbahu, Rav Mana.

Amoraim. Babylon 3950–4200

The Amoraim of Babylon include Rav and Shmuel, Rav Huna and Rabbi Yehudah, Rav Nachman, Rav Chisda, Raba, Rav Yoseph, Rava and Abayee, Rav Papa, Ravina and Rav Ashi.

Geonim. Babylon 4400–4798

Rav Saadyah Gaon
Rav Amram Gaon
Rav Sherira Gaon
Rav Hai Gaon

Rishonim. 4725–5300[43]

Rabbi Yitzhac Alfasi, the Rif (N. Africa, Spain)
Rabbi Shlomo Yitzhaki, Rashi (France)
Baalei Tosafos (France)
Rabbi Moshe ben Maimon, the Rambam (Spain, Egypt)
Rabbi Moshe ben Nachman, the Ramban (Spain)
Rabbi Asher ben Yechiel, the Rosh (Germany, Spain)
Rabbi Yaakov ben Asher, the Baal HaTurim (Germany, Spain)

Acharonim. 5300–present

Rav Yosef Caro (Spain, Turkey, Eretz Yisrael)
Rabbi Moshe Isserles, the Rema (Poland)

---

43. The period of the Rishonim coincides approximately with the period in European history known as the Middles Ages (1000–1500 C.E.). The preceding period in European history is known as the Dark Ages (500–1000 C.E.).

The Maharal of Prague (Austro-Hungarian Empire)
Rabbi Yitzchac Luria Ashkenazi, the Ari Z'L (Eretz Yisrael)
The Vilna Gaon (Poland, Russia)
Rabbi Akiva Eger (Hungary, Prussia)
The Chasam Sofer (Hungary)
The Chofetz Chaim (Poland, Russia)

6. The Ge'ulah Shleimah (the Final Redemption). Messianic Times

The Last Lap

ישעיה יא: ו — Yeshayah 11:6

וגר זאב עם כבש
ונמר עם גדי ירבץ
ועגל וכפיר ומריא יחדו
ונער קטן נהג בם.

And the wolf shall dwell with the lamb,
and the leopard shall lie down with the kid,
and the calf and the young lion and the
    fatling together,
and a little child shall lead them.

ישעיה נט: כ — Yeshayah 59:20
ובא לציון גואל.
And a Redeemer will come unto Zion.

The World at the Time of Mashiach

"The enemies of Hashem will disappear like smoke" (Tehillim 37:20).

"Tzaddikim will rejoice" (Tehillim 107:42).

"The knowledge of Hashem will fill the world like the seas cover the
    ocean" (Yeshayah 11:9).

THREE
Introduction to Lashon HaKodesh

Introduction to Lashon HaKodesh

Lashon HaKodesh is so called because it is the language by which the world was created, as Chazal say: "With this language the world was created."[1]

Hashem gave the letters of Lashon HaKodesh spiritual entity, and by combining the letters of Lashon HaKodesh in different ways, Hashem brought about the spiritual forces of Creation. Thus, when Hashem said, "*Vayehi or* — And there shall be light," He brought together the spiritual forces of the letters *alef, vav,* and *reish* in the Hebrew word "*or*" (אור) to create light.

Lashon HaKodesh is also so called because it is the language of the Torah and the holy *sefarim* of *klal Yisrael*.

1. Lashon HaKodesh in Oral Form

Lashon HaKodesh was the original language of mankind. In Gan Eden, Adam HaRishon spoke Lashon HaKodesh.[2]

Hashem brought all creatures to Adam to see what he would name them. Adam saw the spiritual forces that made up each type and gave it as its name the letters of Lashon HaKodesh that made up that form.

---

1. *Midrash Tanchuma,* Noach 19.
2. Bereishis 2:19 (Rashi).

Thus, when Adam called an ox "shor" (שׁור), he saw that the spiritual forces that made up an ox were brought about through the combination of the letters *shin, vav, reish* (שׁ-ו-ר).

We also learn from this that the name in Lashon HaKodesh of an item is its real name. Its name in any other language bears no relation to the item itself.

As the generations continued, people became dispersed. However, at the time of the Tower of Babel, the people came together, and in order to communicate they spoke a language known to them all — Lashon HaKodesh.[3]

To bring the building to an end, Hashem made them forget Lashon HaKodesh, and they started speaking a multitude of languages. In the confusion the building ended, and the people were dispersed across the world.

However, Lashon HaKodesh remained the language of Avraham Avinu and those descended from him. It was also the language of *klal Yisrael* in Egypt and the language of *klal Yisrael* at the time of the first Beis HaMikdash.[4]

After the destruction of the first Beis HaMikdash, Jews were exiled from Eretz Yisrael. When they returned after seventy years, they brought with them the new languages they had absorbed in exile.

After the destruction of the second Beis HaMikdash, *klal Yisrael* adopted other languages, the languages of the lands of exile.

2. Lashon HaKodesh in Written Form

Each letter of Lashon HaKodesh has its own Divinely ordained form and particular position in the sequence of the *alef-beis*.[5] These are the

---

3. Bereishis 11:1.
4. In Egypt, *klal Yisrael* did not change their Hebrew names, their Hebrew language, and they did not speak *lashon hara* (*Midrash Rabba,* Vayikra 32:5).
5. Talmud: *Shabbos* 104a.

letters that appear in *sifrei Torah* and the scrolls of the Prophets and Holy Writings, and is called *kesav ashuris* (Assyrian script).

For general documents,[6] scribes use a form of lettering similar to *kesav ashuris* but without the same *kedushah* (sanctity). Printers also use a form of lettering similar to the original letters of *sifrei Torah*.

For commentary, printers use a form known as Rashi script.[7] This is so called because it is the form first used by printers for Rashi commentary, and later used for all commentaries, in order to distinguish commentary from the main text.

The cursive or handwritten form of Lashon HaKodesh in use today has been in use for several generations.[8]

Many reference books have been written on Lashon Hakodesh, including the *Oruch* (the first known dictionary, which was written in the eleventh century). The earliest known works on Hebrew grammar come from the period of the Geonim. The best known works on Hebrew grammar were written at the time of the Rishonim by the Ibn Ezra and the Radak and were incorporated into their commentaries on Tanach.[9] Many other *sefarim* have been written on Hebrew grammar through the generations.

---

6. For example, marriage documents.
7. See chart, following page.
8. See chart, following page.
9. The Radak (Rabbi David Kimche 1160-1235).
    The Ibn Ezra, Rabbi Avraham ibn Ezra: biography page 127.

The Twenty-Two Letters of the Alef-Beis

Written Form	Numerical Value**	Name	Rashi Script	Printed Form	Kesav Ashuris (beis Yosef)
k	1	Aleph אָלֶ״ף	ƒ	א	א
ב	2	Beis/Veis בֵּי״ת/בֵי״ת	℥	ב	ב
ג	3	Gimmel גִימֶ״ל	ג	ג	ג
ד	4	Dalet דָלֶ״ת	ר	ד	ד
ה	5	Hei הֵי״א	ה	ה	ה
/	6	Vav וָא״ו	ו	ו	ו
ז	7	Zayin זַיִי״ן	ſ	ז	ז
n	8	Ches חֵי״ת	ט	ח	ח
(	9	Tes טֵי״ת	ט	ט	ט
'	10	Yud יוֹ״ד	׳	׳	׳
ב	20	Chaf/Caf כָ״ף/כַ״ף	כ	כ	בּ*
ל	30	Lamed לָמֶ״ד	ל	ל	ל
N	40	Mem מֵ״ם	מ	מ	מ*
ן	50	Nun נו״ן	)	נ	בּ*
o	60	Samech סָמֶ״ךְ	ס	ס	ס
ર	70	Ayin עַיִי״ן	ע	ע	ע
ə	80	Peh/Feh פֵּי״א/פֵ״א	פ	פ	פ*
ȝ	90	Tzaddi צָדִ״י	ſ	צ	צ*
ק	100	Kuf קוּ״ף	ק	ק	ק
ר	200	Reish רֵי״שׁ	ר	ר	ר
e	300	Shin/Sin שִׁי״ן/שִׂי״ן	ט	ש	ש
ת	400	Taf/Sof תָּי״ו/תָי״ו	ת	ת	ת

* These letters have a different form when they come at the end of a word, and are shown on the next chart.

** In Lashon Hakodesh there are no separate forms for numbers. Rather, the letters themselves have numerical values, known as gematrias, and are used as numbers.

The Five End Letters

Written Form	Numerical Value	Name	Rashi Script	Printed Form	Kesav Ashuris (beis Yosef)
ק		Final Chaf כ״ף פְּשׁוּטָה	ך	ך	ך
ק		Final Mem מֵ״ם סְתוּמָה	ס	ם	ם
/		Final Nun נוּ״ן פְּשׁוּטָה	ן	ן	ן
ן		Final Peh פֵּ״א פְּשׁוּטָה	ף	ף	ף
ק		Final Tzaddi צָדֵ״י פְּשׁוּטָה	ד	ץ	ץ

The Vowels in Lashon HaKodesh

In Lashon HaKodesh the vowels are not separate letters, but signs around the letters, known as *nekudot*.

6	5	4	3	2	1
חוֹלָם	חִירִיק	סֶגוֹל	צֵירֵה	פַּתָח	קָמָץ
וֹ	.	ֶ	ֵ	-	ָ

12	11	10	9	8	7
חֲטַף סֶגוֹל	חֲטַף קָמָץ	חֲטַף פַּתָח	שְׁוָא	שׁוּרֵק	קֻבּוּץ
ֱ	ֳ	ֲ	ְ	וּ	ֻ

FOUR
The Foundation of *Tefillah*

The Foundation of *Tefillah*

1. The Origin of Tefillah (Prayer)

Tzaddikim felt the need to speak to Hashem and did so in their own words.[1]

Avraham initiated praying in the morning, Yitzchak initiated praying in the afternoon, and Yaakov initiated praying in the evening.[2]

When the Torah was given it became a mitzvah to pray to Hashem each day.[3]

2. The Shemoneh Esrei

Prayer in one's own words remained the practice of *klal Yisrael* until the time of the Anshei Knesses HaGedolah, the Men of the Great Assembly, at the beginning of the period of the second Beis HaMikdash. At this time, Jews were returning to Eretz Yisrael, bringing with them the new languages they had absorbed in exile. They were no longer able to express themselves in pure Lashon HaKodesh, and in these circumstances, the Anshei Knesses HaGedolah prepared the first fixed text for *tefillah* in clear and simple Lashon HaKodesh.

---

1. The Talmud calls prayer "the service of the heart" (*Ta'anis* 2a).
2. Talmud: *Berachos* 26b; *Midrash Rabba*, Bereishis 68:11.
3. Rambam, *Hilchos Tefillah* 1:1–2.

They composed a *tefillah* of eighteen *berachos* (blessings), with blessings of praise to start, then requests, and finally blessings of praise and leave-taking to end. The requests were requests for *klal Yisrael* as a nation, but within each *berachah* one could still add one's personal requests.[4] This prayer became known as the Shemoneh Esrei, meaning "the eighteen," the central *tefillah* of the Jewish people.

Later, during the time of the Tannaim, an additional *berachah* was added, called "*Birkas Haminim*." This additional *berachah* was instituted at Yavneh under the leadership of Rabban Gamliel II. The blessing was composed in response to the threats of Jewish heretics — the Sadducees, Boethusians, and Essenes — who tried to lead *klal Yisrael* astray. However, although a blessing was added, the *tefillah* retained the name "Shemoneh Esrei."[5]

In this way, the Shemoneh Esrei became set, the principle part of every *tefillah* of *klal Yisrael*.

Around the Shemoneh Esrei, the Anshei Knesses HaGedolah built the remainder of each *tefillah*, which is said every morning, afternoon, and evening.

3. The Daily Tefillos: Shacharis, Minchah, and Ma'ariv

Shacharis

» In Shacharis the Shema was set before the Shemoneh Esrei in order to fulfill the mitzvah of *kerias Shema* (the saying of the Shema) in the morning.

» A period of preparation is necessary before coming before Hashem in the Shema and Shemoneh Esrei, and thus "*Pesukei D'Zimra*" was set before the Shema.[6]

---

4. One's personal requests can be added to any of the middle thirteen *berachos*, most often to the *berachah* רפאנו — *refa'einu*.

5. Talmud: *Berachos* 28b.

6. "*Zimra*" means "song." Some also explain that the word "*zimra*" is connected to the word "*tizmor*," meaning "to prune," that is, to cut away unwanted thoughts before coming before Hashem in *tefillah*.

» Before *"Pesukei D'Zimra"* our Sages set a section called *"Korbonos,"* which deals with the sacrificial procedure in the Beis HaMikdash. The *korbonos*, or sacrifices, were the principle service of the Beis HaMikdash, and were offered three times each day: morning, afternoon, and evening. The Shemoneh Esrei itself replaces these *korbonos* which, in the absence of the Beis HaMikdash, cannot be brought.[7]

» At the beginning of the morning service, the Anshei Knesses HaGedolah set morning *berachos* (blessings), in which we thank Hashem for our basic needs, which He has restored to us each day.

» After the Shemoneh Esrei was set the concluding part of davening — *"Ashrei," "U'Va L'Tzion," "Aleinu,"* and *"Shir Shel Yom."*

» *Kerias HaTorah* — the reading of the weekly Torah portion — was set for Mondays and Thursdays, when the first section of each week's Torah portion is read.[8]

» Kaddish was set after each main section of prayer.[9]

Thus, the order of the *Shacharis* is the following:
Morning *Berachos*
Korbonos
Kaddish*
Pesukei D'Zimra
Kaddish
Shema
Shemoneh Esrei
Tachanun
Kaddish
Krias HaTorah (on Mondays and Thursdays)
Kaddish

7. The recitation of the section of *korbonos* in *Shacharis* is considered as if one had actually brought these *korbonos* (Talmud: *Ta'anis* 27b.)
8. The mitzvah of *kerias haTorah* on a weekday was instituted by Moshe Rabbeinu so that people would not go for more than three days without hearing Torah (Talmud: *Bava Kama* 82a. Rambam: *Hilchos Tefillah* 12:1).
9. Rambam: *Seder Tefillos*, appendix to *Sefer Ahavah*.

Ashrei
U'Va L'Tzion
Kaddish
Aleinu
Kaddish*
Shir Shel Yom
Kaddish*

* This is the *Kaddish Yasom* (קדיש יתום), Mourner's Kaddish.

Minchah and Maariv

The afternoon and evening *tefillos* were organized in a similar way, around the central pillar of the Shemoneh Esrei. In *Minchah*, the Shemoneh Esrei is preceeded by *Ashrei*, and followed by *Tachanun* (additional supplications) and then *Aleinu*. In *Maariv*, the Shemoneh Esrei is preceeded by the Shema and its blessings, and followed by *Aleinu*.

4. The Other Occasions of Tefillah

Shacharis, *Minchah*, and *Maariv* are the morning, afternoon, and evening prayers, said every day to replace the *korbonos* (sacrifices) of the morning, afternoon, and evening. Every Shabbos and Yom Tov, there is an additional prayer called *Mussaf*, set to replace the *korban mussaf* of the Beis HaMikdash.[10] Only on one other occasion is there any other *tefillah*, the *tefillah* of *Ne'ilah*, which is the concluding prayer of Yom Kippur, said before nightfall.[11]

5. The Different Types of Shemoneh Esrei

Every Shemoneh Esrei is made up by the same first three *berachos* and the same final three *berachos*.

---

10. *Mussaf* means "additional," meaning the additional *tefillah* of Shabbos and Yom Tov.
11. Thus, on Yom Kippur there are five *tefillos*: *Maariv*, *Shacharis*, *Mussaf*, *Minchah*, and *Ne'ilah*.

Every weekday Shemoneh Esrei has, in addition, thirteen middle *berachos*, making nineteen *berachos* altogether.

On Shabbos and Yom Tov, the thirteen weekday *berachos* are replaced by one long central *berachah*, called "*kedushas hayom*," about the sacred nature of the day. Thus, the Shemoneh Esrei of Shabbos and Yom Tov is made up of seven *berachos*.

There is only one occasion when the construction of the Shemoneh Esrei differs. This is the Shemoneh Esrei of *Mussaf* on Rosh HaShanah. This Shemoneh Esrei consists of nine *berachos*, that is, the same first three and the same final three *berachos* as any other Shemoneh Esrei, and in addition three middle *berachos* called "*Malchuyos*," "*Zichronos*," and "*Shofros*."[12]

6. The First Siddur

"*Siddur*" means "order." The first siddur we know of was compiled by Rabbi Amram Gaon over 1,000 years ago at the request of the Jews of Spain, in order to ascertain the correct text and laws of davening. Until then, *tefillos* were said by memory. However, due to the growing dispersion of communities, uncertainties had arisen in davening.[13]

The first siddur was handwritten, containing the daily and weekly prayers of a Jew in order of need, from the time of rising in the morning to the time of going to sleep at night.

As time progressed, other prayers were added to the siddur, in the same order of need through the day and year.

---

12. Each of these middle *berachos* contains ten *pesukim*, three from Torah, three from Kesuvim (Holy Writings), three from Nevi'im (Prophets), and one more from the Torah. These three *berachos* relate to the themes of kingship ("*Malchuyos*"), remembrance ("*Zichronos*"), and shofar blasts ("*Shofros*").

13. At the time of the Beis HaMikdash, the Jewish people lived in the one geographic location of Eretz Yisrael and were unified by the supreme central authority of the Beis HaMikdash, and the Sanhedrin. After the fall of the Beis HaMikdash, Jewish communities developed over far distant lands, and at the time of the Geonim, it was to the Geonim in Babylon that the Jewish people turned to for guidance and leadership.

7. Other Sefarim for Tefillah:
Machzorim, Selichos, and Kinnos

At a later time *machzorim* were compiled, containing the requirements of each Yom Tov. *"Machzor"* means "cycle," implying the yearly prayer needs of a Jew. *Machzorim* were based on the siddur with the addition of *piyutim*.[14]

Selichos and *Kinnos* are also part of the *tefillos* of *klal Yisrael*. *"Selichos"* means "forgiveness." *Selichos* are prayers in which we ask for forgiveness from Hashem. They are said at certain times of year, particularly at the time of Rosh HaShanah and on fast days. *"Kinnos"* means "lamentations." We read *Kinnos* on the evening and morning of Tishah B'Av, when we lament the loss of the Beis HaMikdash and other tragedies that have befallen *klal Yisrael*.

---

14. *Piyutim* are prayers of praise to Hashem composed mainly by the Geonim and Rishonim.

FIVE
Introduction to Torah

1. Written Torah
2. Oral Torah
3. Extension to Written Torah

Introduction to Torah

Torah means "teaching." The Torah teaches us the way of life of a Jew. There are two parts to the Torah: the Written and the Oral Torah.

1. Written Torah

Written Torah consists of the words of Hashem, which Hashem dictated to Moshe Rabbeinu word for word, and which Moshe wrote in the first *sefer Torah*. It is called Written Torah because it was given to be transmitted from generation to generation in written form, every *sefer Torah* being exactly the same as the *sefer Torah* of Moshe Rabbeinu. It is also known as *"Chamishah Chumshei Torah"* (meaning five fifth-parts of the Torah) because it is made up of five individual parts: Bereishis (Genesis), Shemos (Exodus), Vayikra (Leviticus), Bemidbar (Numbers), and Devarim (Deuteronomy).

2. Oral Torah

The mitzvos of Written Torah were given to Moshe Rabbeinu with their explanation.

This explanation is called Oral Torah, because it was given to be transmitted orally, in a chain of transmission that began with Moshe Rabbeinu on Har Sinai.[1]

---

1. For example, Written Torah tells us the mitzvah of sukkah: "In

In later generations Oral Torah was compiled in writing as the Mishnah, and later as the Gemara.

Written Torah

חמשה חומשי תורה
The Five Books of the Torah

Sefer Devarim	Sefer Bemidbar	Sefer Vayikra	Sefer Shemos[3]	Sefer Bereshis
דברים[6]	במדבר[5]	ויקרא	שמות	בראשית[1]
ואתחנן[7]	נשא	צו[4]	וארא	נח
עקב	בהעלותך	שמיני	בא	לך-לך
ראה	שלח	תזריע }	בשלח	וירא
שופטים	קרח }	מצורע }	יתרו	חיי שרה
כי-תצא	חקת }	אחרי מות }	משפטים	תולדות
כי-תבוא	בלק	קדושים }	תרומה	ויצא
נצבים[8] }	פינחס	אמור	תצוה	וישלח
וילך }	מטות }	בהר }	כי תשא	וישב
האזינו	מסעי }	בחקותי }	ויקהל }	מקץ[2]
וזאת הברכה[9]	———	———	פקודי }	ויגש
———	———	———	———	ויחי

There are נ"ד *(fifty-four) parshios of the Torah.*

---

sukkos you shall dwell seven days" (Vayikra 23:42). Oral Torah tells us what a sukkah is — its height, dimensions, materials of construction, and upon whom it is obligatory (Rambam: Introduction to Commentary on the Mishnah).

Notes

Note 1. *Parshas Bereishis:* Parshas Bereishis is the first *parshah* in each new cycle, read the first Shabbos after Simchas Torah.

Note 2. *Parshas Miketz:* Parshas Miketz almost always falls on Shabbos Chanukah.

Note 3. *Sefer Shemos:* The first eight *parshios* of *Sefer Shemos* are known as *Shovevim Tat* (שובבים תת), which is an acrostic of those parshios. The period of these *parshios* is a time particularly suited to teshuvah.

Note 4. *Parshas Tzav:* In a non-leap year *Parshas Tzav* is always the Shabbos before Pesach.

Note 5. *Parshas Bemidbar:* Parshas Bemidbar almost always falls directly before Shavuos.

Note 6. *Parshas Devarim:* Parshas Devarim always falls the Shabbos before Tishah B'Av.

Note 7. *Parshas Vaeschanan:* Parshas Vaeschanan always falls the Shabbos after Tishah B'Av.

Note 8. *Parshas Netzovim:* Parshas Netzovim is always the *parshah* read the Shabbos before Rosh HaShanah. On occasion, both *Parshas Netzovim* and *Parshas Vayelekh* are read the Shabbos before Rosh HaShanah.

Note 9. *Parshas Vezos HaBrachah:* Parshas Vezos HaBrachah is always read on Simchas Torah irrespective of the day of the week. It is the only *parshah* of the Torah that was set to be read on a Yom Tov.

} Indicates which *parshios* can be joined.

Oral Torah

The Six Orders of the Mishnah

1. זרעים (*Zera'im*) _____ Laws of agriculture.
2. מועד (*Mo'ed*) _____ Laws of Shabbos and Yom Tov.
3. נשים (*Nashim*) _____ Laws concerning relationships between men and women.
4. נזיקין (*Nezikin*) _____ Laws of damages and other civil legislation.
5. קדשים (*Kadoshim*) _____ Laws concerning the holy offerings and dietary laws.
6. טהרות (*Taharos*) _____ Laws concerning the purity of the Beis HaMikdash and home life.

There is a mnemonic (memory device) to remember the six Orders of the Mishnah, זמן נקט (*zeman n'kot*), "hold on to time."

3. Extension to Written Torah

After the passing of Moshe Rabbeinu, Written Torah was extended by Nevi'im (the words of the prophets of *klal Yisrael*) and by Kesuvim (the Holy Writings of *klal Yisrael*).

Nevi'im

Nevi'im is divided into two parts: Nevi'im Rishonim and Nevi'im Acharonim. Nevi'im Rishonim relate the history of *klal Yisrael* from the time that *klal Yisrael* entered Eretz Yisrael over a period of 850 years until the destruction of the first Beis HaMikdash. Although Nevi'im Rishonim are historical in nature, they make up part of the prophecies of *klal Yisrael* because they contain warnings of the consequences if *klal Yisrael* stray from the path of Torah.

Nevi'im Acharonim are made up of prophetic visions, some relating to their own time and some to the future of *klal Yisrael*. The Nevi'im Acharonim prophesied from approximately 180 years before the destruction of the first Beis HaMikdash until the first years of the Second Beis HaMikdash.

Kesuvim

Kesuvim (the Holy Writings) of *klal Yisrael* come from a period similar to that of Nevi'im. They extend from Sefer Tehillim (The Book of Psalms) of King David from before the First Beis HaMikdash to Megillas Esther, Daniel, Ezra-Nechemiah, and Divrei HaYamim (Chronicles) at the beginning of the Second Beis HaMikdash.

Nevi'im and Kesuvim together are known as "Nach" (נ״ך), a Hebrew acrostic of the two words. Together with Written Torah, they are known as "Tanach" (תנ״ך), an acrostic of the words "Torah," "Nevi'im," and "Kesuvim."[2]

---

2. There is a way to remember the *sefarim* of Tanach: there are five books of the Torah, eight books of Nevi'im, and eleven books of Kesuvim, each having three more books than the previous one.

The Books of the Prophets & the Holy Writings[1]

Nevi'im — the Books of the Prophets

נביאים ראשונים — The Early Prophets

Yehoshua (Joshua)_____יהושע
Shoftim (Judges)_____שופטים
Shemuel (Samuel) I, II_____שמואל א, ב
Melachim (Kings) I, II_____מלכים א, ב

נביאים אחרונים — The Later Prophets

Yeshaya (Isaiah)_____ישעיה [2]
Yirmiya (Jeremiah)_____ירמיה [3]
Yechezkel (Ezekiel)_____יחזקאל
The Twelve Prophets_____תרי-עשר
  Hoshea (Hosea)_____הושע
  Yoel (Joel)_____יואל
  Amos (Amos)_____עמוס
  Ovadiah (Obadiah)_____עובדיה
  Yonah (Jonah)_____יונה
  Michah (Micah)_____מיכה
  Nachum (Nahum)_____נחום
  Chabakuk (Habakuk)_____חבקוק
  Tzefania (Zephania)_____צפניה
  Chaggai (Haggai)_____חגי
  Zechariah (Zecariah)_____זכריה
  Malachi (Malacai)_____מלאכי

Kesuvim — The Holy Writings

Tehillim (Psalms)_____תהלים
Mishlei (Proverbs)_____משלי
Iyov (Job)_____איוב
The Five Megillas_____חמש מגילות
  Shir HaShirim (Song of Songs)____שיר השירים
  Rus (Ruth)_____רות
  Eichah (Lamentations)_____איכה
  Koheles (Ecclesiastes)_____קהלת
  Esther (Esther)_____אסתר
Daniel (Daniel)_____דניאל
Ezra-Nechemia (Ezra-Nehemia)_____עזרא-נחמיה
Divrei HaYamim (Chronicles)_____דברי הימים א, ב

NOTES:

1. Talmud: *Bava Basra* 14b.
2. ישעיה (Yeshaya) is also known as ישעיהו (Yeshayahu).
3. ירמיה (Yirmiya) is also known as ירמיהו (Yirmiyahu).

SIX
The Transmission of Torah

The Transmission of Torah

At Creation Hashem gave Adam HaRishon six mitzvos as the basis of life. After the Flood, Hashem gave Noach one additional mitzvah: "Do not take a limb from a living animal,"[1] as this was the first time that people were allowed to eat meat as food. These seven mitzvos are known as the *sheva mitzvos b'nei No'ach*, the basis of life for all mankind.

Sheva Mitzvos B'nei No'ach — שבע מצוות בני נח

(Talmud: *Sanhedrin* 56a; Rambam, *Hilchos Melachim* 9:1)

1. Do not bow down to idols _____ עבודה זרה
2. Prohibition of blasphemy _____ ברכת השם
3. Do not murder_____ שפיכות דמים
4. Prohibition of forbidden relations _____ גלוי עריות
5. Do not steal _____ גזל
6. Establish courts of justice _____ דינים
7. Do not take a limb from a living animal ____ אבר מן החי

---

1. Bereishis 9:4.

1. Avraham Avinu

Avraham Avinu was the father of the Jewish people. Avraham came to recognize Hashem. Hashem promised Avraham, "I will make you into a great nation, and I will bless you and make your name great."[2]

Hashem commanded Avraham to perform the mitzvah of bris milah for himself and his offspring. This was the first mitzvah given to the Jewish people alone.

Yaakov Avinu was also given the mitzvah of *gid hanasheh*.[3]

Before the Exodus from Egypt the Jewish people were given their first mitzvos as a nation, concerning Rosh Chodesh (the Sanctification of the New Moon) and Pesach.[4]

2. Matan Torah

At Har Sinai, following the Exodus from Egypt, Hashem declared the *Aseres HaDibros* before the entire Jewish people. Afterwards, Moshe Rabbeinu ascended Har Sinai, and on Har Sinai Hashem taught Moshe the entire Torah, the Written Torah and the Oral Torah — the 613 mitzvos of the Written Torah with their explanations.

Moshe came down from Har Sinai with the *luchos* in his hands on which were written the Ten Commandments in miraculous letters.

Moshe taught Torah to the people — the mitzvos of the Torah and their explanations.[5] Later, Moshe wrote down all the mitzvos of the Torah in the first *sefer Torah*.[6] The explanations of the mitzvos

---

2. Bereishis 12:2.
3. Bereishis 32:33. The mitzvah of *gid hanasheh* is the prohibition of eating the tendon of an animal's thigh.
4. Shemos 12 and 13.
5. Rambam: Introduction to Commentary on the Mishnah.
6. According to one opinion, Moshe Rabbeinu wrote the first *sefer Torah* part by part over the forty years in the *midbar*. According to another opinion, Moshe wrote the first *sefer Torah* all at one time at the end of his life (Talmud: *Gittin* 60a).

of Written Torah, however, were not permitted to be written down. Rather, they were passed down through the generations orally in a chain of transmission that began with Moshe Rabbeinu on Har Sinai.

Before his passing, Moshe gathered all the people and told them that the time had come for him to leave them, and he gave over leadership to Yehoshua before the entire nation.[7]

3. Yehoshua bin Nun. The Elders. The Nevi'im.

The people were led by Yehoshua and his *beis din*, which was the first Sanhedrin. The Sanhedrin was the highest authority in Jewish life, both for the transmission of Oral Torah and for ruling on questions of Jewish law.[8]

Yehoshua and his *beis din* passed on Torah to the Elders.[9] This period was also known as the period of the Judges, as some of the Elders arose as Judges in the land, each passing judgment in his own portion of the land while still being accepted as a leader over the whole people. The Elders and Judges passed on Torah to the Nevi'im (Prophets), who were to lead *klal Yisrael* for the next 600 years. The Nevi'im passed on Torah to the Anshei Knesses HaGedolah, Men of the Great Assembly.

4. The Anshei Knesses HaGedolah

The Anshei Knesses HaGedolah was the chief body of *klal Yisrael* at the beginning of the period of the Second Beis Hamikdash. It was

---

7. Devarim 31:7-8.
8. The Sanhedrin existed from the time of Moshe Rabbeinu until after the destruction of the Second Beis HaMikdash, and was also known as the Beis Din HaGadol. It was made up by seventy-one Elders and, at the time of the First and Second Beis HaMikdash, sat in the *Lishkas HaGazis*, the Chamber of Hewn Stone in the Beis HaMikdash. After the destruction of the Second Beis HaMikdash, the Sanhedrin met in Yavneh under Rabban Gamliel II. However, as persecution intensified under Roman rule it was forced to leave Yavneh and move from place to place in Eretz Yisrael, until finally under Roman rule it was forbidden to meet at all.
9. The Mishnah: *Avos* ch. 1.

made up of 120 Sages, including amongst them the last of the Nevi'im, Chagai, Zechariah, and Malachi. The Anshei Kenesses HaGedolah also included Daniel, Chananiah, Mishoel, Azariah, Ezra the Scribe, Nechemia, Mordechai, and Zerubavel the son of Shealtiel.[10]

The Anshei Knesses HaGedolah were also known as the Scribes, for not only did they pass Oral Torah through their generations, but they also secured Written Torah for *klal Yisrael*. They brought together the prophecies of the Jewish people, finalizing what would be transmitted to future generations as "Nevi'im." They also brought together in collective form the Holy Writings of *klal Yisrael*, known as "Kesuvim." In addition, they ensured that all *sifrei Torah* were written correctly.[11]

Shimon HaTzaddik was one of the last of the Anshei Knesses HaGedolah and the first of the great Sages known as the Tannaim.

5. Tannaim

The Tannaim, meaning "teachers," were the great Sages who led *klal Yisrael* during the critical period of Roman rule at the time of the Second Beis HaMikdash and after its destruction.

After the destruction of the Second Bais HaMikdash the Roman Empire continued to grow stronger and stronger, and the difficulties of life under Roman rule continued to intensify. The numbers of students in the yeshivos decreased, and *klal Yisrael* became dispersed over many lands.[12]

In these conditions of national emergency, our Sages feared for the continued transmission of Oral Torah and took steps to ensure Oral Torah for future generations.

---

10. Rambam: Introduction to Commentary on the Mishnah.
11. There were many more prophecies than those included by the Anshei Knesses HaGedolah in Nevi'im. However, only those prophecies that would be needed for future generations were retained and included (Talmud: *Megillah* 14a).
12. Rambam: Introduction to *Mishneh Torah*.

The work took place under the leadership of Rabbi Yehudah HaNassi, or Rebi, as he was known.[13] Together with the Sages of his generation, Rebi put down in writing a framework for Oral Torah, enough to act as a foundation for future generations. Rebi divided Oral Torah into six sections, called "Orders" — the six orders of the Mishnah.

ששה סדרי משנה
The Six Orders of the Mishnah
and the masechtos (tractates) which make them up[14]

Taharos - טהרות	Kadoshim - קדשים	Nezikin - נזיקין	Nashim - נשים	Moed - מועד	Zeraim - זרעים
כלים	זבחים	בבא קמא	יבמות	שבת	ברכות
אהלות	מנחות	בבא מציעא	כתובות	עירובין	פאה
נגעים	חולין	בבא בתרא	נדרים	פסחים	דמאי
פרה	בכורות	סנהדרין	נזיר	שקלים	כלאים
טהרות	ערכין	מכות	סוטה	יומא	שביעית
מקואות	תמורה	שבועות	גטין	סוכה	תרומות
נדה	כריתות	עדיות	קדושין	ביצה	מעשרות
מכשירין	מעילה	עבודה זרה	———	ראש השנה	מעשר שני
זבים	תמיד	אבות	———	תענית	חלה
טבול יום	מדות	הוריות	———	מגילה	ערלה
ידים	קנים	———	———	מועד קטן	בכורים
עוקצים	———	———	———	חגיגה	———

This great work was the work of a lifetime for Rebi and his Sages, and became known as the Mishnah, meaning "teaching."

Rebi and his Sages had brought together the learning that had

---

13. Rebi was so great in Torah, and in other ways too, that he was called Rabbeinu HaKadosh — our Rabbi, the holy one (Rambam: Introduction to Commentary on the Mishnah).

14. There are ס״ג (sixty-three) *mesechtos* (tractates) of the Mishnah.

been passed down to them through the generations. They had collected, assessed, organized, and written down Oral Torah for use in public for the first time, building a foundation on which future generations would rest.[15]

The leaders in the generations of Tannaim were:

1st generation: Antigonus of Socho

2nd generation: Yose ben Yoezer and Yose ben Yochanan

3rd generation: Yehoshua ben Perachyah and Nitai of Arbel

4th generation: Yehudah ben Tabbai and Shimon ben Shatach

5th generation: Shemayah and Avtalyon

6th generation: Hillel and Shammai[16]

7th generation: Rabban Shimon ben Hillel

8th generation: Rabban Gamliel the Elder

9th generation: Rabban Shimon ben Gamliel

THE DESTRUCTION OF THE SECOND BEIS HAMIKDASH

10th generation: Rabban Gamliel II of Yavneh

11th generation: Rabban Shimon ben Gamliel II

12th generation: Rabbi Yehudah HaNassi[17]

6. Amoraim

After the completion of the Mishnah and the passing of Rebi and his Sages, the generations of Sages who led *klal Yisrael* were known as Amoraim, meaning "interpreters."[18] These Sages learned Oral Torah on the basis of the Mishnah, and throughout their generations,

---

15. Rambam: Introduction to *Mishneh Torah*.
16. The five generations from Yose ben Yoezer and Yose ben Yochanan, until Hillel and Shammai, were known as the "pairs" (*zugos*). The first named was Nasi (leader of *klal Yisrael*), while the second was Av Beis Din (the head of the Sanhedrin). Some differentiate between the *zugos* and Tannaim, referring to Hillel and Shammai as the first generation of Tannaim and those who came before them as *zugos*.
17. Rambam: Introduction to *Mishneh Torah*.
18. After the completion of the Mishnah, no one was allowed to add or subtract from it in any way; the Sages that followed were permitted only to explain and interpret the Mishnah.

they argued and discussed the laws of the Mishnah, adding to the body of Oral Torah by applying the questions of their own time.

Amoraim continued to live in Eretz Yisrael, but persecution under Roman rule intensified, and the deteriorating conditions led many of the last communities to leave the land.

During the lifetime of Rebi the seeds had already been sown for the flourishing of Torah elsewhere. Two of his students, Rav and Shmuel, had founded yeshivos in Babylon, and by the time the last Sages of Eretz Yisrael had to flee the Romans, Babylon already provided a vibrant and flourishing center of Torah. Now Babylon became the spiritual center of the Jewish people, and while the communities of Eretz Yisrael still lasted, there was communication between the great Sages of each land.

The Talmud

About 250 years after the sealing of the Mishnah, Ravina and Rav Ashi, the last of the Amoraim and the leaders of the yeshivos of Babylon, began the task of collating the learning that had been transmitted to them through the generations of Amoraim. This was a lifetime's work for them and their *talmidim*. They brought together the vast learning of the Amoraim in a great work known as the Talmud, or *Talmud Bavli* (the Babylonian Talmud), the monumental central structure of Jewish learning.

In Eretz Yisrael, too, a Talmud had been compiled by the Sages of Eretz Yisrael, called *Talmud Yerushalmi* (the Jerusalem Talmud), which was finalized about 150 years before *Talmud Bavli*. Both *Talmud Bavli* and *Talmud Yerushalmi* were built on the foundation of the Mishnah of Rebi.[19]

---

19. The leaders of the generations of Amoraim in Babylon were 1st generation: Rav and Shmuel, and Rabbi Yochanan; 2nd generation: Rav Huna; 3rd generation: Raba; 4th generation: Rava; 5th generation: Ravina and Rav Ashi (Rambam: Introduction to *Mishneh Torah*).

7. Savoraim

After the passing of Ravina and Rav Ashi, the sages who led *klal Yisrael* in Babylon were known as the Rabbanan Savorai. They were called Rabbanan Savorai (the Ponderers) because they pondered over the teachings of the Amoraim, explaining and interpreting them, and bringing the Talmud to its final form as it has been passed down to us.

This period saw the deterioration of life for the Jews of Babylon. The land that had once provided peaceful settlement and stable conditions now became uncertain. Political conflict in the region led to persecution, and periodically the great yeshivos of Babylon were closed, and about 150 years after the compilation of the Talmud, Arab forces conquered the area.

This conquest, however, brought with it a period of relative peace. The yeshivos of Sura and Pumpedisa were reinstated, and once again students from distant lands came to learn in Babylon.[20]

8. Geonim

This period became known as the period of the Geonim, which was the title given to the leaders of the yeshivos of Babylon at that time.

The Geonim formed the leadership of the Jewish people, and from communities that lived around the Mediterranean travelers came and went on behalf of their communities, seeking advice from the Geonim in an intensive dialogue that became known as *"she'eilos and teshuvos."* This work was incorporated into works of halachah by the Sages of the following generations.

One of the greatest of the Geonim was Rav Hai Gaon, who raised the level of the Babylonian yeshivos to an unprecedented height. However, after his passing 950 years ago, the great yeshivos of Babylon began to decline, after a period of Talmudic leadership of seven centuries, and the Jewish communities of Babylon, beset by fanatical Arab persecution, gradually disappeared.

---

20. The yeshivos of Sura, Pumpedisa, and Nehardea were the greatest of the Babylonian yeshivos.

By now, however, there were communities that had developed further west, in Europe and North Africa. These communities had once looked to Babylon for leadership, but now they were independent Torah centers in their own right and the new focal point of the Jewish world.

Some of these communities had been strengthened by four great Sages, who were captured by pirates in the service of Spanish rulers and offered for ransom to four different Jewish communities along the Mediterranean coast. These four Sages were Rabbi Moshe ben Chanoch, Rabbi Chushiel, Rabbi Shmaryah ben Elchanan, and a fourth Sage whose identity is unknown.

Rabbi Moshe ben Chanoch was ransomed by the Jews of Cordova, Spain; Rabbi Chushiel was ransomed by the Jews of Tunisia, North Africa, and Rabbi Shmaryah ben Elchanan was ransomed by the Jews of Egypt.

Each of these Sages established yeshivos in the lands where they were ransomed and raised a new generation of outstanding scholars, which meant that their communities would be independent Torah centers.

9. Rishonim

Spain was one of the first of the European lands where communities had developed. Jews had lived in Spain for many generations, and later their communities were strengthened by the arrival of Sages from North Africa. The Jews of Spain built communities of great spiritual achievement, wealth, and fame, in a period which became known as the "Golden Age of Spanish Jewry."

One of the greatest Sages of Spain was Rabbi Yitzchak Alfasi, known as the Rif. He was born in Morocco in 1013 but later moved to Spain, where he was regarded as the supreme halachic authority of his time. His greatest work was *Hilchos Rav Alfasi* (*"The Rif"*), in which he abridged the discussions of the Talmud, organizing the vast material that dealt with halachah (Jewish law). He wrote the halachos necessary for Jews in exile, and thus dealt primarily with the sections of the Talmud *Mo'ed*

(Shabbos and Yom Tov), *Nashim* (women), and *Nezikin* (damages).

From Spain, too, came the Rambam, Rabbi Moshe ben Maimon, one of the greatest lights ever to have illuminated the Jewish world. He was born in 1135, although a few years after his birth, his family fled Spain in the face of Muslim persecution, moving through the communities of different lands until they eventually came to Eretz Yisrael. However, they found the land too difficult to sustain life and later moved southwards to Egypt.

Despite these conditions of flight, the Rambam began to write the first of his great works, *Commentary on the Mishnah*. The Rambam also wrote introductions to certain tractates of the Mishnah, which became classic works in their own right.

The Rambam was the spiritual heir of the Rif, learning from *talmidim* of the Rif. The Rambam's greatest work is known as *Mishneh Torah*, or *Yad HaChazakah*, meaning "the mighty hand." In *Yad HaChazakah*, the Rambam codified in a clear and precise structure the vast learning of the Talmud, incorporating the responsa of the Geonim. *Yad HaChazakah* was a brilliant and colossal work which for the first time presented halachah in order of subject. The Rambam based many of his decisions on the Rif, disagreeing with him in only a few cases.[21]

The publication of *Yad HaChazakah* made an immediate impression on the Jewish world, for this was the first time that an all-encompassing work of halachah had been prepared, including the halachah not only for Jewish life in exile, but also for Eretz Yisrael. Some authorities, however, claimed that *Yad HaChazakah* would discourage Jews from learning halachah from the original source of the Gemara.

The Rambam also wrote other great works, including *Sefer HaMitzvos*, in which he enumerated the *taryag* mitzvos of the Torah, and *Moreh Nevuchim* (*Guide for the Perplexed*).

The Rambam was also the spiritual father of his generation, and many communities turned to him in time of distress. The Rambam wrote

---

21. *Mishneh Torah* is known as *Yad HaChazakah* (the mighty hand) because it is made up by fourteen books, *yad* (יד) in Lashon HaKodesh having the numerical value of fourteen.

to these communities, encouraging them to withstand persecution and strengthening them in their faith. One of the most famous of these letters is *"Iggeres Teiman,"* written to the Jews of Yemen.[22]

The Rambam passed away in Egypt in 1204 and was buried in Eretz Yisrael. Of the Rambam it was said, "From Moshe to Moshe, there was no one like Moshe."

Also from Spain came the Ramban, Rabbi Moshe ben Nachman. He was born in 1194 and became one of the greatest sages of his time. The Ramban wrote a commentary on Chumash, which became one of the classic early commentaries, with that of Rashi and the Ibn Ezra.[23] Furthermore, the Ramban wrote a commentary on the Talmud, called "Milchames Hashem," and a work on halachah which was later incorporated into the *Shulchan Aruch* of Rabbi Yosef Caro.

The Ramban was also the fearless defender of his people in the court of the king of Spain, and he helped to strengthen many communities faced with the onslaught of Christian persecution.[24]

In Eretz Yisrael, in his final days, the Ramban wrote his ethical will to his son, known as *"Iggeres HaRamban,"* which has become a classic work of ethical teaching.

During this period of great productivity in Sephardi lands, communities had also developed in France and Germany. In France, in the year 1040, one of the greatest Sages of the Jewish people was born. He was Rabbi Shlomo ben Yitzchak, known as Rashi. He came from a distinguished line of Sages who traced their lineage back to the Royal House of David.

---

22. In the year 1172 the Jews of Yemen were faced with violent persecution. They turned to the Rambam who inspired them and strengthened them — he told them that just as in the past other nations had failed against the Jewish people, so too would this period of persecution pass and peace return to their land.
23. The Ibn Ezra, Rabbi Avraham ibn Ezra, 1089–1164. Biography page 127.
24. The great debate of the Ramban before the King of Aragon, Spain was held in Barcelona, in the year 1263. The Ramban published an account of the debate, but as a result of the debate was forced to leave Spain. He spent the last years of his life in Eretz Yisrael.

Rashi lived during a tragic period for the Jews of Europe, for persecution and expulsion meant that no community was long safe, and towards the end of his life, the Crusades in particular swept through Europe, devastating Jewish communities.

However this was also a productive period in Jewish learning. Rashi established a yeshivah at Troyes, France, which he led for forty years and to which students flocked from all over Europe to learn with the great master. Rashi was the light of his generation — he gave us his classic commentary on Chumash and his colossal commentary on *Talmud Bavli*. In his commentary on Chumash, Rashi drew on his mastery of all areas of Jewish learning. In his commentary on Talmud, Rashi wrote what had been passed down through the generations to his teachers, and from the grandchildren of Rashi came the *ba'alei Tosafos*, the Sages of the following generations who were to bring us further in the understanding of Talmud.

10. Acharonim

In 1488, in the last years of Spanish Jewry, Rabbi Yosef Caro was born. He lived at the end of the period of the Rishonim, and he was one of the first of the Sages known as the Acharonim.

Soon after his birth, his family was forced to flee Spain in face of the Expulsion of 1492. Along with thousands of other Spanish Jews, the family of Rabbi Yosef Caro found refuge in the Turkish Empire, settling in Adrianople.

Rabbi Caro received recognition in his own time and throughout future generations to a degree almost unparalleled in Jewish history. His first great work was his commentary on the *Tur*, the great halachic work of Rabbi Yaakov ben Asher of Germany, written 150 years earlier. Rabbi Caro named this commentary the *Beis Yosef*. In establishing the halachah, Rabbi Caro based himself principally on the opinions of the "three pillars of halachah": Rabbi Yitzchak Alfasi (the Rif), the Rambam, and Rabbi Asher ben Yechiel (the Rosh).

Rabbi Caro also wrote an abridgement of the *Beis Yosef*, in which he presented only the conclusions arrived at in his commentary on the

Tur. He named this work *Shulchan Aruch*, which means "a set table," since it presented halachah in a clear, concise form. Rabbi Caro became known as the "*Mechaber*," that is, the author of the *Shulchan Aruch*.

Rabbi Caro considered the *Shulchan Aruch* an aid for revision of his longer *Beis Yosef*, but within a few years it became the authoritative code for all decisions, while the Gemara remained the original source.

The Four Sections of the *Shulchan Aruch*:

(1) אורח חיים (Orach Chaim) — "The Way of Life": Laws of daily life, Shabbos and Yom Tov.

(2) יורה דעה (*Yoreh Deah*) — "Knowing Knowledge": Laws of kashrus and other areas.

(3) אבן העזר (*Even HaEzer*) — "Stone of Help": Laws of married life.

(4) חשן משפט (*Choshen Mishpat*) — "Breastplate of Justice": Civil and criminal law.

Since Rabbi Caro was a Sephardi, one of the greatest Sages of Europe, Rabbi Moshe Isserles, known as the Rema, compiled annotations to the *Shulchan Aruch* stating Ashkenazi decisions. These annotations soon appeared as an integral part of the *Shulchan Aruch*.[25]

Rabbi Caro passed away in Eretz Yisrael in 1575, where he had settled in his later years.

In the lands of Ashkenazi settlement in Europe during this period, persecution and expulsion had led Jews to seek settlement elsewhere, and Jewish communities had migrated up north-eastward through Europe.

By the end of the sixteenth century, there were large Jewish communities in Eastern Europe, particularly in Poland and later in Russia and other parts of Eastern Europe. Jews established centers of learning and culture in these lands, which would last for five hundred years.

Due to pogroms and persecution from the end of the nineteenth century, Jews fled Eastern Europe in mass exodus that transplanted the seeds of Torah onto new lands.

---

25. The Rema, Rabbi Moshe Isserles, 1520–1572. Biography page 128.

OVERALL STRUCTURE OF JEWISH LEARNING

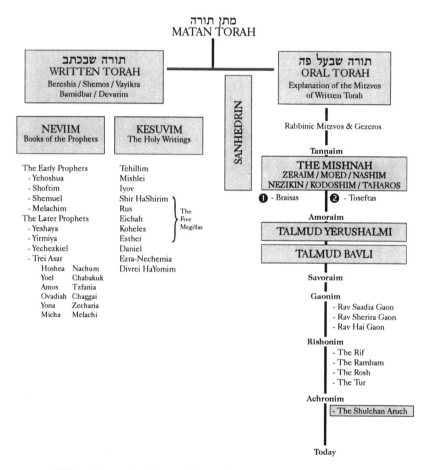

מתן תורה
MATAN TORAH

תורה שבכתב
WRITTEN TORAH
Bereshis / Shemos / Vayikra
Bamidbar / Devarim

תורה שבעל פה
ORAL TORAH
Explanation of the Mitzvos
of Written Torah

NEVIIM
Books of the Prophets

KESUVIM
The Holy Writings

SANHEDRIN

Rabbinic Mitzvos & Gezeros

Tannaim

The Early Prophets
- Yehoshua
- Shoftim
- Shemuel
- Melachim
The Later Prophets
- Yeshaya
- Yirmiya
- Yechezkiel
- Trei Asar

Tehillim
Mishlei
Iyov
Shir HaShirim
Rus
Eichah
Koheles
Esther
Daniel
Ezra-Nechemia
Divrei HaYomim

The
Five
Megillas

Hoshea   Nachum
Yoel   Chabakuk
Amos   Tzfania
Ovadiah   Chaggai
Yona   Zecharia
Micha   Melachi

THE MISHNAH
ZERAIM / MOED / NASHIM
NEZIKIN / KODOSHIM / TAHAROS

❶ - Braisas   ❷ - Toseftas

Amoraim

TALMUD YERUSHALMI

TALMUD BAVLI

Savoraim

Gaonim
- Rav Saadia Gaon
- Rav Sherira Gaon
- Rav Hai Gaon

Rishonim
- The Rif
- The Rambam
- The Rosh
- The Tur

Achronim
- The Shulchan Aruch

Today

The Foundation of Judaism

❶ Kaballah

❹ Midrash

❺ Haggadah Shel Pesach

❻ Machshava

❼ Mussar

❽ Tefillah

❶ & ❷ Braisas – meaning "outside material." Toseftas, meaning "additional material." Braisas and Toseftas were halachic material of the Tannaim which Rebi and his Sages chose to omit from the Mishnah and which were preserved by their pupils in separate works.

❸ Kaballah – the principle work of Kaballah is regarded as the Zohar HaKodosh written by the Tanna Rabbi Shimon bar Yochai זצוק״ל.

❹ Midrash – Midrash means exposition or explanation. The midrashim are the words of Chazal (the Tannaim & Amoraim) explaining the books of Tanach, in particular, Chumash, and are divided into two main types, Midrash Aggadah and Midrash Halachah. On Chumash the principle midrashim are as follows:

Midrash Aggadah: Midrash Rabbah; Midrash Tanchuma
Midrash Halachah: Mechilta (on Shemos); Toras Kohanim (Sifra on Vayikra); Sifri (on Bamidbar & Devarim)

❺ Hagaddah Shel Pesach – The Hagaddah is the sefer that Chazal gave us to lead us through the order and mitzvos of Seder night. Jews have been observing the Seder each year since the first Seder in Mitzraim. Later, a specific text, the Hagaddah Shel Pesach, was provided for Seder night, set at the time of the Tannaim and Amoraim. The earliest text of the Hagaddah is found in the Mishnah itself (Pesachim, ch. 10).

❻ Machshava – Jewish thought and philosophy. For example: Emunos VeDeos by Reb Saadiah Gaon; Sefer HaKuzari by Rabbi Yehuda HaLevi; the Rambam – parts of Commentary on the Mishnah and Mishneh Torah, and Moreh Nevuchim; Derech HaShem by Rabbi Moshe Chaim Luzzato; Nefesh HaChaim by R. Chaim of Volozhin; The Nineteen Letters by Rabbi Samson Raphoel Hirsch.

❼ Mussar – Learning regarding conduct and relationship between man and Hashem, and man and his fellow man. The principle works of mussar include: Chovos HaLevovos by Rabbeinu Bachya; Sefer HaYashar attributed to Rabbeinu Tam; Shaarei Teshuva by Rabbeinu Yona; Menoras HaMaor by Rabbi Yitzhak Abohab; Maalas HaMidos; Ohrhos Tzadikim; Tomer Devora by Rabbi Moshe Cordavero; Mesilas Yesharim by Rabbi Moshe Chaim Luzzato.

❽ Tefillah – The classic commentaries on tefillah include the Avoudraham; Siddur of Rabbi Yaakov Emden; Siddur HaGra-Ishe Yisroel; Siddur Otzer HaTefillas.

SEVEN
Halachah

Halachah

1. THE JEWISH YEAR

(1) The Year

The Jewish calendar is a lunar calendar, based on the cycle of the moon around the earth. This cycle takes twenty-nine and a half days, so the months are alternately twenty-nine or thirty days long, except for Cheshvan and Kislev, which can be either twenty-nine or thirty days. There are twelve months in a regular year and thirteen months in a leap year.

The Torah requires that the Jewish festivals fall not only on the same date each year but also at the same season. Thus, the lunar cycle needs to be maintained in line with the solar cycle, which determines the seasons. However, the solar year of 365 days is eleven days longer than twelve lunar cycles. Accordingly, an extra month, Adar II, is added to the year, so making a leap year seven times every nineteen years. In this way, the co-incidence between the two cycles is maintained.

(2) The Week

The days of the week are called *yom rishon, yom sheini, yom shelishi, yom revi'i, yom chamishi, yom shishi*, and *Shabbos Kodesh*. Thus, the days of the week lead up to and revolve around Shabbos.[1]

(3) The Day

The day begins at *alos hashachar*, when the first rays of light appear on the horizon in the morning. This is followed by *neitz hachamah*, the moment when the crescent of the sun appears on the horizon. The sun moves up from the horizon and when the sun reaches halfway across the sky it is called *chatzos hayom*, or midday. The sun continues to move across the sky, eventually setting in the west. The moment the sun has entirely submerged below the horizon is called *shekias hachamah*, or "sunset." As the sun continues to sink further below the horizon, the sky continues to darken and it becomes night, the start of a new halachic day.

Sha'os Zemaniyos

The period of daytime is divided into twelve equal parts, called *sha'os zemaniyos* (seasonal hours). During the summer months, when daylight lasts for more than twelve hours, a "seasonal hour" will be more than one actual hour. During the winter months, when daylight lasts less than twelve hours, a "seasonal hour" will be less than one actual hour.[2]

According to the Vilna Gaon[3] the period of the day is calculated between *neitz hachamah* and *shekias hachamah*. However, according to the Magen Avraham,[4] the period of day is calculated between *alos*

---

1. We count each day of the week in the *Shir Shel Yom* at the end of *Shacharis*, leading up to Shabbos Kodesh.
2. Thus, if *neitz hachamah* is at 6:00 A.M., and *shekias hachamah* is at 6:00 P.M., daylight will last for 12 hours, and a seasonal hour will also be one hour long.
   If *neitz* is at 8:00 A.M. and *shekiah* at 4:00 P.M., daylight will last for 8 hours, and thus one seasonal hour will be 40 minutes long.
   If *neitz* is at 4:00 A.M. and *shekiah* is at 8:00 P.M., daylight will last for 16 hours, making one seasonal hour 80 minutes long.
3. The Vilna Gaon, Rabbi Eliyahu of Vilna. Biography page 128.
4. The Magen Avraham, Rabbi Avraham Gombiner. Biography page 129.

hashachar and *tzeis hakochavim* (when three small stars can be seen in the night sky).

(4) The Halachic Times of Day and Year

» *Alos hashachar* — "the coming up of the morning." Also called *amud hashachar* — "the pillar of the morning," or daybreak.

» *Techilas zeman tzitzis, tefillin, v'kerias Shema* — "the earliest time to put on tzitzis and tefillin and to say Shema in the morning."

» *Neitz hachamah ("neitz")* — the appearance of the crescent of the sun on the horizon in the morning. This time follows *alos hashachar* by about seventy-two minutes, depending on the time of year.[5]

» *Sof zeman kerias Shema shel shacharis* — "the latest time for saying Shema in the morning," which is at the end of three seasonal hours, or one-quarter of the day.[6]

» *Sof zeman tefillas shacharis* — "the latest time for davening the morning Shemoneh Esrei," which is at the end of four seasonal hours, or one-third of the day.[7]

» *Chatzos hayom v'halailah* — six seasonal hours or "halfway through the day or night."

---

5. *Neitz* is the moment when the crescent of the sun first appears on the horizon in the morning. According to a second opinion, *neitz* is the moment when, from where one is situated, one can first see the crescent of the sun. This second opinion of *neitz* is called *"neitz hachamah hanireh"* (the sun's crescent which is seen) and may give a different time for *neitz* if, for example, one is in a valley or on top of a mountain.

6. Thus, if *neitz hachamah* is at 8:00 A.M. and *shekias hachamah* at 4:00 P.M., a seasonal hour will be 40 minutes, and *sof zeman kerias Shema* will be at 10:00 A.M.

7. Thus, if *neitz hachamah* is at 8:00 A.M. and *shekias hachamah* at 4:00 P.M., a seasonal hour will be 40 minutes, and *sof zeman tefillah* will be at 10:40 A.M.

» *Minchah gedolah* — This is half an hour after *chatzos hayom*, which is six and a half seasonal hours into the day. *Minchah gedolah* is the earliest time to daven *Minchah* in the afternoon.

» *Minchah ketanah* — This is nine and a half seasonal hours into the day, after which is the preferred time to daven *Minchah*.

» *Plag haminchah* — "halfway through that time of *Minchah*." This is halfway between the time of *Minchah ketanah* and *shekias hachamah*, that is, 10¾ seasonal hours into the day. This is the earliest time to bring in Shabbos on Friday afternoon.

» *Shekias hachamah* — This is the moment the entire sun has disappeared below the horizon in the evening. The period from *shekias hachamah* until night is called *bein hashmashos* — "between the suns" or twilight.

» *Zeman hadlakas haneiros b'erev Shabbos Kodesh* — Although Shabbos begins at *shekias hachamah*, we do not wait until this time before refraining from weekday activities. Rather, we add a period to the start of Shabbos, called *tosefes Shabbos*, which sets the time for lighting the Shabbos candles and the latest time for *melachos* before Shabbos. The period of *tosefes Shabbos* can be up to forty minutes before *shekias hachamah*.

» *Zeman ma'ariv u'zeman motza'ei Shabbos Kodesh* — The time for davening *Maariv* on a weekday and the time for davening *Maariv* after Shabbos. The earliest time for davening *Maariv* on a weekday is normally about thirty minutes after *shekias hachamah*. However, after Shabbos we wait an additional period after *shekias hachamah* before davening *Maariv*, which is when three small stars can be seen in the night sky (*tzeis hakochavim*). This period will vary according to time of year and place; in Eretz Yisrael this period will be about forty minutes after *shekias hachamah*. According to Rabbeinu Tam,[8]

---

8. Rabbi Yaakov ben Meir, "Rabbeinu Tam," 1100–1171. Biography page 130.

Maariv is davened on *motza'ei Shabbos* seventy-two minutes after *shekias hachamah.*

» *Zeman molad halevanah* — "the birth of the new moon." The moon renews itself every twenty-nine days, twelve hours, and forty-four minutes. The specific time of the "*molad*" is announced on the Shabbos morning preceding Rosh Chodesh.[9]

» *Sof zeman kiddush levanah* — "the latest time to sanctify the new moon." The latest time to sanctify the new moon is halfway through the month, after which time the moon begins to wane.

» *Tekufos* — "seasons." The cycle of the earth around the sun is divided into four parts called "*tekufos*" or "seasons": autumn, winter, spring, and summer. Certain changes in *tefillah* depend on the season.[10]

> The halachic times of day which are most required in practice are *alos hashachar; neitz hachamah; sof zeman kerias Shema; sof zeman tefillos Shacharis; chatzos hayom; shekias hachamah;* and *zeman ma'ariv u'zeman motza'ei Shabbos Kodesh.*

---

9. This announcement is followed by the announcement of the actual day of the week on which Rosh Chodesh falls.

10. For example, the prayer for rain in the Shemoneh Esrei (*"tal u'matar"*) is recited from the sixtieth day of the autumn *tekufah* until Pesach.

The Jewish Year				
Month	**Yom Tov**	**Other Important Days**	**Special Shabbosos**	**Other Fast Days**
Tishrei[1] – תשרי *30 days*	*Rosh HaShanah:* 1 & 2 Tishrei[2] *Yom Kippur:* 10 Tishrei[3] *Sukkos:* 15-21 Tishrei[4] *Shemini Atzeres:* 22 Tishrei	Aseres Yemey Teshuvah — the 10 days of Teshuvah Chol-Moed Sukkos/ Hoshanah Rabah	Shabbos-Shuvah[5] Shabbos Chol-Moed Sukkos	Tzom Gedaliah: 3 Tishrei[6]
Cheshvan[7] – חשון *29 or 30 days*				
Kislev – כסלו *29 or 30 days*	*Chanukah:* from 25 Kislev for 8 days[8]		Shabbos Chanukah	
Teves – טבת *29 days*				Asarah B'Teves: 10 Teves[9]
Shevat – שבט *30 days*		Tu-B'Shevat[10]	Shabbos Shirah[11] Shabbos Shekalim[12]	
Adar – אדר *29 days*	*Purim:* 14 Adar[13]		Shabbos Zocher[14] Shabbos Parah[15] Shabbos HaChodesh[16]	Taanis Esther (Fast of Esther): 13 Adar[17]
Nissan – ניסן *30 days*	*Pesach:* 15-21 Nissan[18]	Chol-Moed Pesach	Shabbos HaGadol[19] Shabbos Chol-Moed Pesach	
Iyar – אייר *29 days*		Pesach Sheni[20] Lag BaOmer[21]		
Sivan – סיון *30 days*	*Shavuos:* 6 Sivan[22]			
Tammuz – תמוז *29 days*				Shivah Asar B'Tammuz: 17 Tammuz[23]
Av – אב (Menachem Av) (מנחם אב) *30 days*		Tu-B'Av: 15 Av[24]	Shabbos Chazon Shabbos Nachamu[25]	Tisha B'Av: 9 Av
Ellul[26] – אלול *29 days*				

Notes

1. Tishrei — Tishrei is the first month of the year in the counting of the years, whereas Nissan is the first month of the year in the cycle of the months of the year (Talmud: *Rosh HaShanah* 2a).

2. Rosh HaShanah — Rosh HaShanah is *Yom HaDin*, the Day of Judgment, when each Jew is judged and his *din* sealed. For many, judgment is not sealed until Yom Kippur. Rosh HaShanah and Yom Kippur are known as the Yomim Noraim, the Days of Awe. The period between Rosh HaShanah and Yom Kippur is called the עשרת ימי תשובה, the Ten Days of Repentance, when each Jew is required to improve himself (*Shulchan Aruch, Orach Chaim* 603).

3. Yom Kippur — The Day of Atonement. Those whose judgment was not sealed on Rosh HaShanah are sealed on Yom Kippur. On Yom Kippur, in addition to the prohibition of eating and drinking, it is forbidden to wash oneself, or to anoint oneself, or to wear leather shoes (Talmud: *Yuma* 73b).

4. Sukkos — In Eretz Yisrael, Sukkos is from 15-21 Tishrei, one day Yom Tov followed by six days of Chol HaMoed. The days of Chol HaMoed are days of semi-Yom Tov, and the last day of Chol HaMoed Sukkos is called Hoshanah Rabbah. Hoshanah Rabbah is the final day for the sealing of judgment that began on Rosh HaShanah, and on it we recite extra prayers and supplications before Hashem. Shemini Atzeres is a separate Yom Tov falling on 22 Tishrei, that is immediately following Sukkos. In Eretz Yisrael, Simchas Torah also falls on Shemini Atzeres. Simchas Torah is a *siyum* or celebration at the completion of the cycle of reading the Torah each year.
Outside of Eretz Yisrael, Sukkos falls 15-22 Tishrei. The 22nd and 23rd of Tishrei are also Shemini Atzeres, and Simchas Torah falls on 23 Tishrei.

5. Shabbos Shuvah — Shabbos Shuvah is the Shabbos before Yom Kippur, so called because of the first word of the *haftorah* of that week: "Return, Israel, to Hashem your God" (...אלקיך, שובה ישראל עד ה׳) (Hosea 14).

6. Tzom Gedaliah — The fast of Gedaliah. This fast marks the murder of Gedaliah ben Achikom, who was the governor of Eretz Yisrael appointed by Nevuchadnetzar after the destruction of the First Beis HaMikdash. With the murder of Gedaliah, any possibility of renewed Jewish life in Eretz Yisrael came to an end.

7. Cheshvan — Cheshvan is the second month in the year, and the eighth after the count of the months from Nissan. Cheshvan is also known as Marcheshvan, because no festivals occur during it, *mar* meaning bitter. Another reason that this month is known as Marcheshvan is because the rainy season begins during it, *mar* meaning a drop of water.

8. Chanukah — Chanukah marks the miracles in the victory over the Greeks during the time of the Second Beis HaMikdash, over 2,000 years ago. Shabbos Chanukah is the Shabbos which falls during Chanukah. When Chanukah begins on Friday night, there are two Shabbosos during Chanukah, the first day and the last day of Chanukah.

9. Asarah B'Teves — The Fast of 10 Teves marks the beginning of the siege of Jerusalem by Nevuchadnetzar of Babylon, which eventually lead to the destruction of the First Beis HaMikdash. This is the only fast in the Jewish year that can fall on a Friday.

10. Tu B'Shvat — Tu B'Shvat (15 Shevat) is the new year for trees, when trees are judged for their produce (Talmud: *Rosh Hashanah* 2a). On Tu B'Shvat we are accustomed to eat species of fruit, particularly the seven types of fruit for which the Torah praises the Land of Israel (Devarim 8:8).

11. Shabbos Shirah — This is the Shabbos of *Parshas Beshalach* which includes the "Song at the Sea," *shirah* meaning song (Shemos 15:1–19).

12. Shabbos Shekalim — This is the Shabbos before Rosh Chodesh Adar or on Shabbos Rosh Chodesh Adar when we read the portion of the Torah concerning the donation of half-shekels to the Beis HaMikdash. This donation was used to pay for the communal offerings of the Beis HaMikdash. At the time of the Beis HaMikdash the announcement to make the donation was made at the beginning of Adar, and thus we read this portion on the Shabbos before Rosh Chodesh Adar.

13. Purim — Purim marks the victory of the Jews of Persia over 2,300 years ago, under Mordechai and Esther. In cities that were walled at the time of Yehoshua bin Nun, Purim falls on the 15th Adar and is called Shushan Purim.

14. Shabbos Zachor — *"Zachor"* means "remember." This is the Shabbos before Purim

when we fulfill the mitzvah to remember what Amalek did to us when we came out of Egypt. The reading of this portion falls on the Shabbos before Purim, because on Purim the battle was against Haman who was a descendant of Amalek.

15. Shabbos Parah — This is the Shabbos before Shabbos Parshas HaChodesh, when a special reading is made regarding the *parah adumah*, the red heifer. Its ashes were mixed with water and used to purify any Jew who was *tamei mes* (impure through touching a dead person) before he would be able to come up to Yerushalayim to offer the *korban Pesach*. Although at present, we are not able to bring the *korban Pesach*, we read *Parshas Parah*, *zecher leMikdash*, in remembrance of the time of the Beis HaMikdash.

16. Shabbos HaChodesh — This is the Shabbos before the beginning of Nissan or the Shabbos falling on Rosh Chodesh Nissan, when we make a special reading of the Torah which proclaims Nissan as the first month of the year and to alert people to prepare for Pesach.

17. Taanis Esther (The Fast of Esther) — This fast falls on 13 Adar, the day before Purim, and marks the fast of three days called by Esther before going to King Achashveiros to ask for a favor to save *klal Yisrael*.

18. Pesach — In Eretz Yisrael Pesach falls 15-21 Nissan, whereas outside of Eretz Yisrael Pesach falls 15-22 Nissan. The intermediate days of Pesach are called Chol HaMoed, which are days of Semi-Yom Tov.

19. Shabbos HaGadol — This is the Shabbos before Pesach when we commemorate the day just prior to the Exodus, when the Israelites took a lamb in order to slaughter it four days later. The lamb was a holy animal to the Egyptians, and it was a miracle that they were unable to prevent it being taken and slaughtered.

20. Pesach Sheini — "The Second Pesach." Pesach Sheini falls on 14th Iyar, exactly one month after the *korban Pesach* was brought. At the time of the Beis HaMikdash a person who was unable to bring the *korban Pesach* on 14th Nisan could bring it on Pesach Sheini. Today, some are accustomed to eat matzah on Pesach Sheini.

21. Lag BaOmer — During the seven weeks from Pesach to Shavuos we count the *omer* each day — *sefiras haomer* meaning "the counting of the *omer*." We do so to fulfill the mitzvah of the Torah that from the 2nd day of Pesach — the *omer* offering of new barley was brought in the Beis HaMikdash — forty-nine days are to be counted until Shavuos. The *sefirah* period became a time of semi-mourning because of different tragedies that occurred during that period. However, the 33rd day of the *omer* is a day of rejoicing called Lag BaOmer (לג בעומר), ל״ג having the numerical value of 33.

22. Shavuos — Shavuos is the Yom Tov which marks the time of the giving of the Torah, and is called *Zeman Matan Toraseinu* (זמן מתן תורתנו) — the Time of the Giving of the Torah. In Eretz Yisrael Shavuos falls on 6 Sivan, whereas outside of Eretz Yisrael Shavuos falls on 6 and 7 of Sivan.

23. Shivah Asar B'Tammuz — This fast marks several events, particularly the breaching of the walls of Jerusalem by the Romans, leading to the destruction of the Second Beis HaMikdash. With the fast of Shivah Asar B'Tammuz we begin a period of mourning called "The Three Weeks," which ends on Tishah B'Av, the day of the destruction of the Beis HaMikdash.

24. Tu B'Av — "The Fifteenth of Av." This is the last day of planting for the year with reference to the *shemitah* cycle, and the day when the cutting of the wood for the Beis HaMikdash was completed each year. It was also the day of forgiveness for the generation of the *midbar* (wilderness) and a time of rejoicing in *klal Yisrael*.

25. Shabbos Chazon — Shabbos Chazon is the Shabbos before Tishah B'Av, and is so called after the first words of the *haftorah*: "The vision of Isaiah, son of Amos..." ("חזון ישעיהו"). (Isaiah 1).
   Shabbos Nachamu is the Shabbos after Tishah B'Av, and is so called after the first words of the *haftorah*: "Comfort, comfort My people ("נחמו נחמו עמי") (Isaiah 40).
   The *haftorah* of Shabbos Nachamu is the first of seven *haftoros*, called the "Seven of Consolation," which are read during the seven weeks between Tishah B'Av and Rosh HaShanah.

26. Ellul — Ellul is the last month of the year, before Rosh HaShanah. Although Hashem is close to His people at all times, the month of Ellul in particular is a time for *teshuvah*, for during Ellul Hashem is particularly close to His people, as it is written: "I am to My beloved and My beloved is to Me" ("אני לדודי ודודי לי") (*Shir HaShirim* 6, 3).

2. SHABBOS

Shabbos Kodesh is the great sign and the covenant that Hashem gave the Jewish people.[11]

Shabbos Kodesh is also the foundation of *emunah* (faith), for by keeping Shabbos we are acknowledging that Hashem created the world in six days and rested on the seventh day, and that we are His servants, obligated to do His will.

Furthermore, it is written, "If Israel would keep two Shabbosos fully they would be redeemed straight away" (Talmud: *Shabbos* 118b).

(1) The Torah

The Torah places two obligations upon a person with regard to Shabbos: to remember the Sabbath day, as it says, "Remember the Sabbath day,"[12] and to refrain from performing any labor on the Sabbath, as it says, "Guard the Sabbath day."[13] However, with the exception of the prohibition of kindling a fire, the Torah does not state what constitutes labor on Shabbos.

(2) The Thirty-Nine *Av Melachos* of Shabbos

The Torah prefaces the section dealing with the construction of the Mishkan with a repetition of the prohibition of labor on Shabbos.[14] From this juxtaposition of these *parshiyos* (Torah portions), our Sages determined that the prohibited forms of work on Shabbos were those necessary for the construction of the Mishkan and its components.[15]

---

11. *Sefer Chayei Adom*, Introduction to Hilchos Shabbos by Rabbi Avraham Danzig. Biography page 130.
12. Shemos 20:8. The mitzvah of remembering the Sabbath day is fulfilled through the recitation of the *tefillos* of Shabbos and Kiddush.
13. Devarim 5:12.
14. Shemos 35:1–3. The Mishkan (Tabernacle) was the portable home for the *luchos* and the center of Divine worship which the Israelites built in the *midbar* (wilderness).
15. Talmud: *Shabbos* 97b.

Our Sages categorized these forms of work into thirty-nine specific categories, known as the "*av melachos*," which are the actual activities in the construction of the Mishkan. These *melachos* are listed in the Mishnah.[16]

The Thirty-Nine Av Melachos of Shabbos

1. Sowing	זורע
2. Ploughing	חורש
3. Reaping	קוצר
4. Gathering	מעמר
5. Threshing	דש
6. Winnowing	זורה
7. Sorting	בורר
8. Grinding	טוחן
9. Sifting	מרקד
10. Kneading	לש
11. Baking (Cooking)	אופה/מבשל
12. Shearing	גוזז
13. Whitening	מלבן
14. Combing	מנפץ
15. Dyeing	צובע
16. Spinning	טוה
17. Mouting the Warp	מסך
18. Setting the Heddles	עושה שני בתי נירין
19. Weaving	אורג
20. Removing threads	פוצע
21. Tying	קושר
22. Untying	מתיר
23. Sewing	תופר
24. Tearing	קורע

continued on the next page

---

16. Mishnah: *Shabbos* 7:2; *Talmud: Shabbos* 73a.

25. Trapping	צד
26. Slaughtering	שוחט
27. Skinning	מפשיט
28. Salting/tanning	מולח/מעבד[17]
29. [Tracing lines]	[שרטוט]
30. Smoothing	מוחק (עור)
31. Cutting	מחתך
32. Writing	כותב
33. Erasing	מוחק (כתב)
34. Building	בונה
35. Demolishing	סותר
36. Extinguishing	מכבה
37. Kindling	מבעיר
38. Striking the final blow	מכה בפטיש
39. Transferring from domain to domain	הוצאה

(3) *Toldos*

The Torah intended to prohibit not only the specific work done in the construction of the Mishkan, but also those types of work whose nature was intrinsically the same. Those related types of work are known as "*toldos*," or "extensions" of the *av melachos*. Both *av melachos* and *toldos* have the same level of *issur* on Shabbos; both are Torah prohibitions.[18]

---

17. The list of *melachos* in the Mishnah (*Shabbos* 7:2) includes salting hides and tanning as separate *melachos*. The Talmud (*Shabbos* 75b) states that these are really the same *melachah*, and inserts שרטוט, "tracing lines," as the twenty-ninth *melachah*.

18. For example, an *av melachah* is the prohibition of *kosev* (writing two or more letters of any alphabet). The *toldos* of *kosev* include the prohibition of drawing pictures on Shabbos.

(4) Rabbinic Mitzvos and *Gezeiros*

The Torah also instructed our Sages to build a "fence" around the Torah to protect people from the prohibitions of the Torah, as it says, "And you shall keep that which I have entrusted you to guard,"[19] which the Talmud explains is an admonition to take measures to protect the precepts of the Torah.[20]

Thus, our rabbis enacted additional laws, called *mitzvos d'rabbanan*, where they protect the Torah by instructing that an act be done, and *gezeiros*, where they protect the Torah by forbidding an act.

With regard to Shabbos, there are two *mitzvos d'rabbanan* — *kavod Shabbos* (to honor Shabbos) and *oneg Shabbos* (to enjoy Shabbos).[21] These mitzvos are based on the words of the Prophets.[22]

However, in regard to Shabbos most rabbinic laws are *gezeiros*, an example of which is the prohibition of carrying in a *karmelis*.[23]

(5) Additional Rabbinical Enactments

Even if one avoided the forbidden *melachos* of Shabbos, Shabbos could still seem similar to a weekday in certain respects. Thus, the Sages enacted further prohibitions not connected with actual *melachos*, in order to reinforce the concept of rest on Shabbos and to enhance the sanctity of the day. These prohibitions include *shevus*, *muktzeh*, and *uvda d'chol*.[24]

---

19. Vayikra 18:30.
20. Talmud: *Yevamos* 21a.
21. Rambam, *Hilchos Shabbos* 30:1.
22. Yeshaya 58:13–14.
23. On Shabbos there are three principle types of areas: a *reshus hayachid*, a *karmelis*, and a *reshus harabim*. A *reshus hayachid* is a small, walled area; a *karmelis* is a small open area; and a *reshus harabim* is a wide public area. The Torah permits carrying in a *reshus hayachid* and a *karmelis*, but prohibits carrying in a *reshus harabim*. However, as a *karmelis* could easily resemble a *reshus harabim*, the rabbis enacted a decree, or *gezeirah*, prohibiting carrying in it and gave it the name *karmelis*.
24. *Shevus* — the prohibition of activities which are not a *melachah* but which detract from one's rest on Shabbos. *Muktzah* — the prohibition of moving certain objects on Shabbos. *Uvda d'chol* — the prohibition of activities so

(6) The Halachah

The halachah, meaning "the way to go," that is, the precise way to keep Shabbos, has been taught to us by the *poskim* of each generation, particularly the Rishonim and Acharonim.

3. KASHRUS

"For I am the Lord your God; sanctify yourselves and be holy, for I am Holy."[25]

This is the foundation of the laws of kashrus, to achieve a level of holiness.

One who is careful with kashrus brings holiness and extra purity to his soul (*nefesh*) and cleanses himself for Hashem.[26]

Furthermore, one who is careful regarding kashrus will merit Divine assistance to elevate himself still further in holiness, as it is written: "One who sanctifies himself a little, the heavenly powers help him to sanctify himself a lot" (Talmud: *Yuma* 39a).

(1) Kashrus in the Source of Food

(i) *Food of the ground* growing in and on the ground (for example, vegetables and grains) — all are kosher.[27]

(ii) *Food that grows from the ground* (for example, fruit of the tree) — all are kosher.[28]

---

that one's conduct on Shabbos should be different from one's conduct on a weekday. Included in this category is the prohibition of running on Shabbos (other than for purposes of a mitzvah) and the prohibition of talking about one's weekday activities on Shabbos.

25. Vayikra 11:44.
26. Rambam: *Sefer Kedushah, Hilchos Ma'acholos Assuros* 17:32.
27. That is, all types are kosher. This food may nevertheless be rendered non-kosher if grown in an incorrect manner. See "Kashrus in the Growth of Food" below.
28. See note 27 above.

(iii) *Food from other forms of life.*

» *Land life* — The permitted animals are those that both chew the cud and have a split hoof. These are principally cattle (which provide beef and veal), sheep (which provide mutton and lamb), and goats.[29]

» *Sea life* — only those with fins and scales are permitted.[30]

» *Fowl* — birds of prey are forbidden. Permitted fowl are principally chicken and turkey.[31]

» *Lower forms of life* (insects and creeping life) — mainly forbidden.[32]

Forbidden animals live off other forms of life or are scavengers. But all kosher animals live off vegetation.

An animal or fowl is called a *treifah* (meaning "torn") if upon inspection after slaughtering it was found to have a wound which meant it could not have lived unaided for another twelve months. An animal is called a *neveilah* if it died in any other way than *shechitah*. However the word *treif* is a term which has become commonly used to describe any type of non-kosher food.

(2) Kashrus in the Growth of Food

» *Chadosh* — "new." The prohibition of eating from the new crop of grain until the *korban omer* is brought in the Beis HaMikdash, at Pesach time each year.[33]

---

29. Vayikra 11:3.
30. Vayikra 11:9.
31. The Torah states the names of the forbidden fowl (Vayikra 11:13–19). The Talmud tells us the signs of kosher fowl. But as we are uncertain which are in fact the kosher fowl, we eat only fowl that we know to be kosher, from knowledge passed down to us through the generations, principally chicken and turkey.
32. Vayikra 11:20, 23.
33. *Shulchan Aruch, Yoreh Deah* 293.

» *Arlah* — "uncircumcised." This is the prohibition of eating produce of trees less than three years old. This applies to fruit of Eretz Yisrael, and to fruit from outside of Eretz Yisrael if it is known to be definitely *arlah*.[34]

» *Kelayim* — "mixtures." This is the prohibition of planting different types of seeds side by side within a certain area.[35]

» *Shemittah* — "rest." This is the prohibition of growing or working on produce of the field during the seventh year. *Shemittah* applies only to Eretz Yisrael.

(3) Kashrus in the Preparation of Food

» *Shechitah* — "slaughter." This is the slaughtering of animals and fowl. After *shechitah* the *shochet* examines the animal or fowl for internal defects and removes any forbidden parts.

» *Melichah* — "salting," or kashering. After *shechitah*, any remaining blood is removed by salting or grilling.

» *Basar v'chalav* — "meat and milk." It is written in the Torah three times not to cook a kid in the milk of its mother.[36] From this we learn the three restrictions that the Torah puts on a Jew regarding the mixture of milk and meat: not to cook them together; not to eat them together; and not to benefit from them being cooked together.[37] Therefore we do not cook milk and meat together, or use the same utensils for milk and meat. We also wait a time period between eating dairy foods and meat.[38]

---

34. *Shulchan Aruch, Yoreh Deah* 294.
35. The prohibition of *kelayim* also applies to areas other than food, for example the prohibition of *sha'atnez* (wearing wool and linen in one garment) and the prohibition of working different types of animals under the same yoke (such as an ox and a mule).
36. Shemos 23:19, 34:26; Devarim 14:21.
37. *Shulchan Aruch, Yoreh Deah* 87.
38. After eating meat we customarily wait up to six hours before eating milk. *Shulchan Aruch, Yoreh Deah* 89.

» *Hafrashas terumos u'ma'asros* — "the separation of *terumos* and *ma'asros*." These are two types of separation taken from food grown in Eretz Yisrael. Food from which *terumos* and *ma'asros* has still to be taken is called *tevel* and is forbidden to be eaten.[39]

» *Bedikas tola'im* — "checking for insects." It is a Torah prohibition to eat any swarming creatures, such as insects, flies, worms, or their eggs.[40] Thus we check vegetables and other foods for signs of infestation.

» *Hafrashas challah* — "the separation of challah." This is the separation of a small portion of dough when kneading a large quantity for bread.[41]

(4) Kashrus in the Vessels We Use

» *Tevilas keilim* — "the immersion of vessels in a mikveh." Vessels of metal and glass made by a gentile or ever owned by a gentile require immersion in a mikveh before they can be used by a Jew. In this way they are brought into "*kedushas Yisrael*," the holiness required of vessels used by a Jew.[42]

» *Hachsharas keilim* — "kashering." Vessels that have become *treif* (for example, dairy utensils accidentally used for meat, or vice versa) need to be cleansed by a process called kashering.

---

39. *Terumos* and *ma'asros* are "gifts" that were given to the *kohanim* (priests) and Levi'im for their service during the time of the Beis HaMikdash. In the absence of the Beis HaMikdash, these special portions are not consumed but are wrapped and disposed of before the food they came from can be eaten.
40. Vayikra 11:20, 23.
41. Challah means "a loaf of bread" — that is, making one small loaf and giving it to the *cohen* when baking a larger quantity for yourself. The bread we bake for Shabbos became known as *challah*, since Shabbos was when a sufficient quantity of bread to fulfill the mitzvah of taking challah was normally baked. In the absence of the Beis Hamikdash this portion is not given to the *cohen* but is either burnt or wrapped up and disposed of.
42. *Shulchan Aruch, Yoreh Deah* 120.

This is done either by immersing in boiling water (*hagalah*) or through burning with a blowtorch (*libun*). Both *libun* and *hagalah* extract the *treif* substance from the vessel: *hagalah* extracts the *treif* substance from the walls of the vessel into the boiling water, and *libun* burns off the *treif* remains.[43]

(5) Decrees of the Sages

At the time of the Anshei Knesses HaGedolah, our Sages saw that *klal Yisrael* were to spend many years in exile amongst the other nations. In order to prevent social mixing, they made several decrees with regard to food.[44]

» *Bishul akum* — "food cooked by a gentile." A Jew is forbidden to eat food where the cooking was done completely by a gentile, even if all the ingredients are kosher and were cooked in kosher vessels.[45]

» *Pas akum* — "bread baked in a gentile bakery." The Sages forbade eating bread baked in a gentile bakery, even if all the ingredients are kosher, if bread baked by a Jew is readily available.

» *Stam yayin* — "plain wine." Drinking wine touched by a gentile is prohibited. In addition, there is the Torah prohibition of *yayin nesech*, "poured wine." This is the prohibition of drinking the wine of a gentile in case it was intended for a gentile religious service.[46]

---

43. *Shulchan Aruch, Orach Chaim* 451.
44. *Shulchan Aruch, Yoreh Deah* 112.
45. *Shulchan Aruch, Yoreh Deah* 113. The prohitibion of *bishul akum* does not apply to food usually eaten raw (for example, most fruits) and also does not apply to food which is not usually eaten as part of a meal (for example, chocolate). However, the prohibition of *bishul akum* does apply to food usually served as part of a main meal.
46. *Shulchan Aruch, Yoreh Deah* 123.

The Sages also forbade certain foods from a gentile because they could easily come to include non-kosher ingredients:[47]

» *Chalav akum* — "milk from a gentile source."

» *Gevinas akum* — "cheese produced by a gentile."

> Many of the requirements of kashrus mentioned above will be provided for before coming to the consumer, as long as the food has been prepared under good rabbinic supervision.

(6) Shabbos and Yom Tov

Some of the thirty-nine *melachos* of Shabbos apply to the preparation of food on Shabbos and Yom Tov, such as *dash* (threshing), *borer* (selecting), *tochen* (grinding), *lash* (kneading), and *afiah/bishul* (baking/cooking).

Yom Tov is different from Shabbos in that cooking for one's needs on Yom Tov is permitted on a flame that existed before Yom Tov, whereas on Shabbos it is completely forbidden to begin cooking.

Pesach

On Pesach there are additional prohibitions. It is prohibited to eat *chametz* in any form, whether on its own or in combination with other food.[48]

---

47. *Shulchan Aruch, Yoreh Deah* 115.
48. *Chametz* is one of the five species of grain — wheat, barley, rye, oats, and spelt — which has come into contact with water for eighteen minutes or longer, causing it to rise.

Shabbos and Yom Tov, kashrus and *tefillah*, are mitzvos at the foundation of a Jewish home and the framework of our lives.

» *mitzvos at the foundation of a Jewish home:* because from them one will come to keep the rest of the Torah.

» *and the framework of our lives:* because they set the pattern of each day, each week, each month, and each year.

Each year is not a repetition of the previous year, but another cycle in a progression that leads to the time of Mashiach. May it be His Will that he comes soon in our days. Amen. *Selah.*

תם ונשלם שבח לא-ל בורא עולם.

Biographies

1. Rabbeinu Yonah of Gerona

Rabbeinu Yonah was born in Gerona, Spain, in 1180 and was a contemporary of both the Rambam (Rabbi Moshe ben Maimon) and the Ramban (Rabbi Moshe ben Nachman). He was one of the giants of holiness and Torah that we call the Rishonim. His most famous *sefer* is the classic work *Sha'arei Teshuvah* (*The Gates of Repentance*). In addition, he wrote a commentary on the Talmud and on *Sefer HaHalachos* of the Rif. Other works include a commentary on *Pirkei Avos* (*Sayings of the Fathers*), a commentary on Mishlei (the Book of Proverbs), and *Sha'arei HaAvodah* (*The Gates of Service*). Towards the end of his life, Rabbeinu Yonah set out to travel to Eretz Yisrael, but was detained by different communities of Spain, who beseeched him to stay as their spiritual leader. He died in Toledo, Spain, in 1263.

2. Rabbi Samson Raphael Hirsch

Rabbi Samson Raphael Hirsch was born in Hamburg, Germany, in 1808 at a time when Reform Judaism was making inroads into German Jewry. Hirsch was educated in Hamburg under the Chacham Rabbi Isaac Bernays and later in Mannheim under Rabbi Yaakov

Ettlinger, following a path that would lead him to become one of the leaders of Torah Jewry in Western Europe. In 1836 Hirsch published his first famous work, *The Nineteen Letters*. This was followed by the publication of *Horeb* in 1838 and later his other great works — a commentary on Chumash, a commentary on Sefer Tehillim (Psalms), a commentary on *Pirkei Avos* (*Sayings of the Fathers*), on Mishlei (the Book of Proverbs), and on the siddur. In 1851, Hirsch resigned his position as Chief Rabbi of Moravia and Austrian Silesia to take up the call of a group of families in Frankfurt to become their spiritual leader. Hirsch saw this as a Divine call to a historic mission, to which he had dedicated his life. In Frankfurt, Hirsch began by establishing Orthodox schools, then the other institutions of an Orthodox community, gradually building a community which became the model for Orthodox communities across Germany and in other lands, firmly establishing Hirsch at the forefront of the struggle in Germany against Reform. Hirsch died in Frankfurt in 1888.

3. Rabbi Moshe Chaim Luzzato

Rabbi Moshe Chaim Luzzato, the Ramchal, was one of the spiritual giants we call the Acharonim. He was born in Padua, Italy, in 1707, although he later moved to Amsterdam. He published his first *sefer* at the age of seventeen, and over the next few years he wrote many other works. In 1734, he published *Da'as Tevunos* (*The Knowing Heart*) and *Kelalei Chachmas Emes* (*The Rules of Wisdom and Truth*). At this time he also wrote one of his principal works, *Derech Hashem* (*The Way of God*). In 1740, the Ramchal published his most famous work, *Mesilas Yesharim* (*The Path of the Upright*), the classic *sefer* of the steps to spiritual perfection. At the end of his life, the Ramchal settled in Eretz Yisrael, where he died in 1746.

4. Rabbi Yehudah HaLevi

Rabbi Yehudah HaLevi was born in Spain in 1080 and was a student of the Rif (Rabbi Yitzchak Alfasi) and the Ri Migash (Rabbi Yoseph ibn Migash). He was one of the greatest of all Hebrew poets, whose work is characterized by the deep longing of Israel in exile for redemption and for Zion. He composed the *kinah* for Tishah B'Av "*Tzion Halo Sish'ali*" ("O Zion will you not enquire..."). He also composed Shabbos *zemiros* (songs) such as "*Yom Shabbason.*" In addition, his work was incorporated into our *tefillos* for certain times of year. His *sefer* the *Kuzari*, is a classic sefer on the fundamentals of Judaism. The *Kuzari* was first written in Arabic, the language of the Jews of Spain at the time, but before long it was translated into Hebrew and then into other languages. In his later years, Rabbi Yehudah HaLevi journeyed to Eretz Yisrael, where he died in 1145.

5. Rabbi Avraham ibn Ezra, the Ibn Ezra

Rabbi Avraham ibn Ezra was born in Toledo, Spain in about the year 1089, and was one of the giants of Torah called the Rishonim. At different times of his life he lived in Spain, Italy, France, and also in London, England. In addition, he traveled to the Jewish centers of the east — Africa, Egypt, Babylon, Persia, and Eretz Yisrael. Wherever he traveled he was enthusiastically received, and in France the Tosafist Rabbeinu Tam accorded him great honor. His opinion is brought in Tosafos (Talmud: *Rosh HaShanah* 13a).

In his youth the Ibn Ezra was already recognized as a great *paytan*, who wrote poems of strength and comfort to *klal Yisrael*. Included in his work is the Shabbos *zemer* "*Tzamah Nafshi.*" The Ibn Ezra also wrote works of philosophical and ethical teaching, *chiddushim* on Talmud, and many works on Hebrew grammar. One of his greatest works is his commentary on Torah, which ranks as one of the great classic commentaries on the Torah. His other great works include his commentary on Nevi'im (Prophets) and Kesuvim (the Holy Writings).

In 1160, the Ibn Ezra was once again in France. He passed away in about the year 1164, although the actual date and place of his passing is unknown.

6. Rabbi Moshe Isserles

Rabbi Moshe Isserles, the Rema, was one of the greatest leaders of Polish Jewry in the sixteenth century. He was born around the year 1520 in Cracow, Poland, and when still a young man, was appointed to the *beis din* of Cracow. He also founded a yeshivah in Cracow which drew students from all over Poland. His great work *Darkei Moshe* is a commentary on the *Tur*, the halachic work of Rabbi Yaakov ben Asher of Germany, written 150 years earlier. The commentary of the Rema is parallel to that of Rabbi Yoseph Caro on the *Tur*. However, it included further decisions of the Ashkenazi rabbis of France, Germany, and Poland. Based on *Darkei Moshe*, the Rema compiled annotations to the *Shulchan Aruch* of Rabbi Caro, a work which he called *Mapah* (*Tablecloth*) to indicate that his annotations were meant only to complement the *Shulchan Aruch*. These annotations soon appeared as an integral part of the *Shulchan Aruch*. The Rema passed away on Lag BaOmer in 1572.

7. Rabbi Eliyahu of Vilna, the Vilna Goan

Rabbi Eliyahu of Vilna, known as the Vilna Gaon, or simply as "the Gaon," was one of the greatest lights to have illuminated the Jewish world for centuries.

He was born in the year 1720, and lived most of his life in Vilna, Lithuania. He studied mostly on his own, having contact with only a few close *talmidim*. Yet he had the profoundest influence on his time and on all succeeding generations.

He mastered all areas of learning at a young age. Yet he refused to accept any rabbinical post or position, and instead, attired in *tallis* and *tefillin*, devoted his days and nights to learning Torah.

His works include commentaries on Torah and Tanach, commentaries on the Mishnah, commentaries and annotations on *Talmud Bavli* and *Talmud Yerushalmi*, commentaries on the midrashim, on Tosephta, *Shulchan Aruch*, and on the Zohar. Most of these works were based on notes of the Gaon that he made in his own *sefarim* and on his oral teachings to his *talmidim*, and have come down to us as recorded by his *talmidim*.

The Gaon also undertook the daunting task of establishing the most accurate possible text of Talmud and Midrashim by systematically eliminating the distortions that had crept into the texts of copyists over the centuries. Thus the Gaon restored the words of Chazal to their full form.

Not only was the Gaon a genius in all areas of learning, but in the conduct of his personal life he pursued personal self-perfection.

Towards the end of his life the Gaon set out to settle in Eretz Yisrael. Although he did not fulfill his plans, his *talmidim* were inspired through him to settle there, and a decade after his passing, *talmidim* of the Gaon were amongst the first to settle in Eretz Yisrael in recent times.

The Gaon passed away on the third day of Chol HaMoed Sukkos, the nineteenth of Tishrei, 1797, and two hundred years after his passing, he is still revered as the great light who raised the level of *klal Yisrael*.

8. Rabbi Avraham Gombiner, the Magen Avraham

Rabbi Avraham Gombiner, the "Magen Avraham," was one the greatest Sages of seventeenth-century Europe. He was born in Gombin, Poland in 1634, at a turbulent time for the Jews of Europe, for soon afterwards the Chmielnicki massacres broke out, in which his parents were killed.

Rabbi Avraham achieved lasting renown through his monumental work *Magen Avraham*, which is a commentary on all sections of the *Shulchan Aruch Orach Chaim*. *Magen Avraham* was first published in 1692, and became together with *Turei Zahav* one of the classic commentaries on *Shulchan Aruch Orach Chaim*, printed in all editions of the *Shulchan Aruch* today.

Besides *Magen Avraham*, Rabbi Avraham also wrote other works, the most famous of which is called *Zayis Ra'anan*, which is a commentary on Midrash *Yalkut Shimoni*. In addition Rabbi Avraham wrote *Shemen Sasson*, which is a commentary on parts of the Torah. He also wrote a short commentary on *Tosefta* order *Nezikin*. His other works include a commentary on *Shulchan Aruch Even HaEzer*, and *chiddushim* on tractates *Zevachim* and *Menachos* of the Talmud. The Magen Avraham passed away in Kalish, Poland in 1682.

9. Rabbi Yaakov ben Meir, Rabbeinu Tam

One of the greatest of the grandsons of Rashi was Rabbi Yaakov ben Meir, known as Rabbeinu Tam, meaning "the pure one." Born in the year 1100, his mother was one of Rashi's daughters and his oldest brother, Shmuel, known as the Rashbam, was also one of the greatest Sages of his time.

Already in his youth, Rabbeinu Tam achieved renown as a great scholar, and when he founded a yeshivah in France, some of the greatest students of his time came to learn there.

In his yeshivah Rabbeinu Tam delivered his talmudic discourses, which included examination of Rashi's commentary as well as comparisons between parallel texts of the Talmud. This work became the basis of the annotations on the Talmud called Tosafos, meaning "additions" — that is, additions to the basic commentary of Rashi. In this way the yeshivah became established as the center of the early Tosaphists.

Not only was Rabbeinu Tam considered the greatest Talmudic Sage of his generation, but he was also the leading halachic figure of his time. Some of his work on halachah was collected in *Sefer HaYashar*, which includes responsa written by Rabbeinu Tam in answer to the many questions that were asked of him from the communities of different lands.

The life of Rabbeinu Tam did not escape tragedy, for in 1146 the Crusaders entered his town, desecrating his home and wounding him, leaving him to only narrowly escape with his life.

Rabbeinu Tam passed away in Troyes, France, in 1171.

10. Rabbi Avraham Danzig

Rabbi Avraham Danzig, the Chayei Adom, was born in the year 1748, and was to become one of the greatest sages of his time, serving on the *beis din* of Vilna during the time of the Vilna Gaon. His principle works are *Chayei Adom* and *Chachmas Adom*, which were an abridgment of the *Shulchan Aruch*, *Orach Chayim*, and *Yoreh Deah*, which became basic halachah *sefarim* for much of Eastern European Jewry. Rabbi Avraham Danzig passed away in 1820.

Bibliography

Authorized Daily Prayer Book. England: United Synagogue, 1990.

Bergman, Rabbi Meir Zvi. *Gateway to the Talmud*. New York: Mesorah Publications, Ltd., 1985.

Danzig, Rabbi Avraham. *Chayei Adam*. Jerusalem: Eshkol.

Danzig, Rabbi Avraham. *Chachmas Adam*. Jerusalem: Levin-Epstein.

Elias, Rabbi Joseph. *The Haggadah*. New York: Mesorah Publications, Ltd., 1995.

Falk, Rabbi Pesach Eliahu. *Halachic Guide to the Inspection of Fruits and Vegetables for Insects*. Gateshead: Falk, 1985.

Ganzfried, Rabbi Shlomo. *Kitzur Shulchan Aruch*. Bnei Brak: Frankel.

The Early Acharonim. New York: Mesorah Publications, Ltd., 1989.

The Rishonim. New York: Mesorah Publications Ltd., 1991.

Ganz, Yaff. *Sand and Stars*. Vol. I and II. New York: Shaar Press, 1994.

HaLevi, Rabbi Yehudah. *The Kuzari*. New York: Metzudah, 1986.

Hirsch, Rabbi Samson Raphael. *Horeb*. New York: Soncino, 1994.

Hirsch, Rabbi S. Raphael. *The Nineteen Letters*. Jerusalem: Feldheim Publishers, 1995.

Isaacs, Jacob. *Our People*. New York: Merkos L'Inyonei Chinuch, 1991.

Kitov, Eliyahu. *The Book of Our Heritage*. Jerusalem: Feldheim Publishers, 1988.

Loewe, Rabbi Yehudah (The Maharal of Prague). *The Mitzvah Candle*. Jerusalem: Feldheim Publishers, 1993.

Luzzato, Rabbi Moshe Chaim. *Derech Hashem (The Way of God)*. Jerusalem: Feldheim Publishers, 1988.

Maimon, Rabbi Moshe ben (Rambam). *Introduction to the Mishnah*.

Maimon, Rabbi Moshe ben (Rambam). *Introduction to Sefer Mada (The Book of Knowledge)*.

Munk, Rabbi Michael. *The Wisdom in the Hebrew Alphabet*. New York: Mesorah Publications, Ltd., 1990.

Munk, Rabbi Dr. Elie. *The World of Prayer*. Jerusalem: Feldheim Publishers, 1990.

Posen, Rabbi Yaakov Yechezkiel. *Kitzor Hilchos Shabbos*. Jerusalem: Feldheim Publishers, 1989.

Spice and Spirit. New York: Lubavitch Women's Cookbook Publications, 1992.

Spier, Arthur. *The Comprehensive Hebrew Calendar*. Jerusalem: Feldheim Publishers, 1986.

Taubenhaus, Ephraim. *Giants of the Spirit*. Israel: Sinai, 1981.

The Mishnah-Shabbos. New York: Mesorah Publications, Ltd., 1988.

Wagshall, Rabbi S. *The New Practical Guide to Kashrus*. Feldheim 1991.

Wein, Rabbi Berel. *Echoes of Glory*. New York: Shaar Press, 1991.

Wein, Rabbi Berel *Herald of Destiny*. New York: Shaar Press, 1993.

Wein, Rabbi Berel *Triumph of Survival*. New York: Shaar Press, 1990.

ל״נ

ר׳ משה בן ר׳ אהרן ז״ל
Moshe Saffer

נלב״יע י״ד תמוז תשמ״א

ת׳ נ׳ צ׳ ב׳ ה׳

— — — — —

ל״נ

החבר יעקב ב״ר אברהם ז״ל
Rev. Jacob Lopes Salzedo

נלב״יע י״ט כסלו תשמ״ג

ת׳ נ׳ צ׳ ב׳ ה׳

לע"נ
ר' שלמה ב"ר יהודה ז"ל
Stuart Young

נלב"ע כ"ד מנחם אב תשמ"ו

ת' נ' צ' ב' ה'

‒ ‒ ‒ ‒

לע"נ
מרת יעטא בת ר' שמחה ע"ה
Yvonne Aaronberg

נלב"ע י"ז אלול תשע"ך

ת' נ' צ' ב' ה'

ל"נ

ר׳ יוחנן בן ר׳ ברוך יהודה ז"ל

Jack Wertenteil

נלב"ע ב׳ שבט תשי"א

וזוגתו

מרת שרה בת אהרן ע"ה

Sarah Wertenteil

נלב"ע י׳ סיון תשמ"ה

ת׳ נ׳ צ׳ ב׳ ה׳

לע״נ

ר׳ מרדכי ב״ר חיים זאב ז״ל

Max Spark

נלב״יע ד׳ אייר תשט״ו

וזוגתו

מרת שרה רחל בת ר׳ אליעזר ע״ה

Rose Spark

נלב״יע כ״ב אלול תשל״ח

ת׳ נ׳ צ׳ ב׳ ה׳

ל״נ

ר׳ שלמה ב״ר רפאל הכהן ז״ל

Solomon Aaronson

נלב״ע י״ט תשרי תשכ״ב

וזוגתו

מרת הינדא בת ר׳ משה הכהן ע״ה

Hinda Aaronson

נלב״ע ח׳ תשרי תשל״ד

ת׳ נ׳ צ׳ ב׳ ה׳